BOB GIBSON TELLS HIS
LIFE STORY IN A SPORTS BOOK
YOU WON'T WANT TO MISS

The youngest of seven children, Bob Gibson grew up fatherless in a ghetto in Omaha, Nebraska. A sickly child, he developed himself into a fine athlete—but soon found that being as good as other boys wasn't enough. He had to be better . . . because he was black.

FROM GHETTO TO GLORY

TO GLORY

THE STORY OF BOB GIBSON

BY BOB GIBSON WITH PHIL PEPE

POPULAR LIBRARY · NEW YORK

To my daughters
RENEE AND ANNETTE
and a future
that is brighter
than the past

BOB GIBSON

INTRODUCTION

I ached all over. Every muscle in my body was sore, so sore I felt as if I had been in a gang fight and was the only one in my gang. I thought I would fall flat on my face with exhaustion right there on the pitcher's mound in front of 35,000 people.

I thought I could not possibly continue, but I knew I would try. I had come this far. I could not quit now. This game meant too much to me . . . to us . . . the St. Louis Cardinal ball club. It meant the world championship . . . and $8,000 per man. To me it meant an opportunity to salvage a frustrating season.

From the middle of July to the first week in September my contribution to the team had been exactly zero. I sat by idly, my right leg in a cast, and watched with mixed emotions of pride and frustration while my teammates ran away from the rest of the National League.

I had come back to pitch in only five games before the World Series and now I was trying to complete my third Series game in nine days and wondering where I would get the strength to make another pitch.

It was the seventh game of the 1967 World Series against the Boston Red Sox, who had surprised us all by winning the fifth and sixth games and extending the Series to the limit.

We took a commanding 7–2 lead into the ninth inning, but we had all been around long enough to know that you take nothing for granted in the game of baseball.

Carl Yastrzemski started the inning with a single, but I got Ken Harrelson to hit into a double play and now I had to get just one more out to win the thing. The batter was George Scott. The count went to 2–2. Wearily I looked in to get the sign from Tim McCarver. He wanted a slider.

I wound up and put everything I had left in the pitch. It came in high, but with pretty good stuff on it, and Scott swung at it. He missed. It was over. The Cardinals were 1967 world champions of baseball.

The next thing I knew Tim was pounding me on the back and I was being swallowed up by my teammates, who seemed to come from all directions to reach the mound. They half carried, half dragged me off the field and into the clubhouse, which was bedlam.

Everything happened so fast after that . . . the endless whirl of parties and parades and appearances . . . that I hardly had time to think about all that was happening to me. Later, when I did think about it, I could not help having misgivings. I felt guilty about my happiness at a time when there was so much trouble in the world. With all that was going on, it made my little game of baseball suddenly seem so insignificant.

The name of the book is "From Ghetto To Glory," but I am not so sure about the "Glory," although I can write volumes on the "Ghetto." I suppose, in the generally accepted standard of success in our society, there is "Glory" in winning three World Series games; in attaining a measure of financial security. But I am not satisfied with those accomplishments. I will not be satisfied until all people in all countries are treated equally: until any person, regardless of the color of his skin, can go where he pleases, eat where he pleases, work where he pleases, live where he pleases. I will not be satisfied until the fight for civil rights is won. Then, and only then, will there be Glory.

Perhaps it is a rationale, but I take comfort in the thought that a man must do his thing, no matter what it may be. Mine is throwing a baseball. That is my tool. It is what I used to escape the ghetto and it is what I must use to make whatever contribution I can. I only hope that I do not misuse it. All a man can do, after all, is use what he has to the best of his ability.

In a world filled with hate, prejudice, and protest, I find that I too am filled with hate, prejudice, and protest. I hate phonies. I am prejudiced against all those who have contempt for me because my face is black and all those who accept me only because of my ability to throw a baseball. I am not proud of that ability. It is not something I earned or acquired or bought. It is a gift. It is something that was given to me—just like the color of my skin.

I protest against all the half-truths and untruths that have been said about me and I protest against those who try to get me to say something controversial about someone else.

I remember the day we won the 1964 National League pennant. A reporter came to me in the dressing room and asked me what I thought about the statement by Philadelphia manager Gene Mauch that the Cardinals would never win the pennant as long as Bob Gibson pitched for them. I said I thought nothing about it. Not anger and not outrage. Nothing. I said I did not have time to worry about Gene Mauch; that I had my job to do and he had his job to do.

That reporter was trying to get me to say something about Gene Mauch. Maybe Mauch made that statement and maybe he didn't, I don't know. But as long as I didn't hear him say it, I could not comment on it. I make it a policy never to comment on anything I hear secondhand and never to go on assumptions.

Another thing that annoys me is the untruths magazines insist on writing about me. I get tired of reading the same things over and over. One of the errors I read most frequently is that a recurrence of my childhood asthma attacks forced me to quit playing with the Harlem Globetrotters and concentrate on baseball. It makes interesting reading and I hate to ruin a good story, but that is not how it was.

On the pages that follow I tell it like it is. All of it.

CHAPTER 1 *NO WAY OUT*

It begins for me on November 9, 1935, a day in which official city records show nine children came into the world in Omaha, Nebraska. Had I known then what I was getting myself into—and if I had any choice in the matter—I might have been tempted to say, "No, thank you."

I was fatherless.

I was poor.

I was black.

I never knew my father. I have never seen a picture of him. He died three months before I was born and when I came along my mother was left with seven children to raise on the meager wages she was paid for her job in a laundry.

The first home I knew was a four-room wooden shack on Omaha's North Side. It was old and dilapidated and poorly heated, but it was home. There were two bedrooms. My oldest sister, Beulah, slept with my mother in one bed and I slept on an army cot. My brothers slept in the other room.

It was not as unpleasant for us as it seems, but I will always remember that house, without affection, as the house where I was bitten on the ear by a rat.

Later we moved to the government housing project and even though it was in the ghetto, it was a step up in class because we had heat and electricity.

It was there that I first sensed I was different from other kids. The housing project was segregated. I was very small when we moved there, but the first thing I noticed was that the Negroes lived on one side of the project and the whites lived on the other side. At first it was something I took for granted and accepted as the natural order of things. But when they start calling you names you begin noticing it, and you realize the reason they are calling you names is that you are a different color.

We fought a lot in the housing project. The fights were part of our daily life. They were fundamentally racial, but not entirely so, because we had a few white kids on our side. Glenn Sullivan was one. Another was Dick Mackie and another was Jack Myers. They played with us and they fought with us when we had these big fights, which lasted until some grown-ups broke it up and we'd stop fighting and go home and start all over the next day. We were young and the fights and insults were something we could pass over easily. As you get older, the insults pierce deeper and you are less forgiving.

When we were not fighting we were competing against one another. There was a courtyard in the project and during the summer we had footraces there. Late into the night we would race. Around the courtyard, up the street and back again, running like mad, over and over until we were tired. Then we would go home and go to bed.

It always seemed to me that the Negro kids in the project spent more time in sports and participating in things like this than the average white kid. The white kid had more things to do. He could go to the movies, but we could not. We never had the money. So we ran footraces and played ball because there was nothing else to do, unless you wanted to go out and get in trouble. Many did.

For about three or four years after I started playing pro ball I would go to the state penitentiary when the season ended and speak to the inmates. Some of them were guys I had grown up with. We ran around together and got in little scraps, but as I got older I drifted away from them because I was occupying my time with baseball and basketball. Some of them didn't care much for sports, so they continued on the same path and ended up in prison while I ended up in baseball. There is little difference between us . . . in background, in environment, in home life . . . and seeing them in prison, I kept thinking that if it were not for sports I might have been right there alongside them.

There were about twice as many whites in the project as there were Negroes, which may be surprising. We weren't the only ones who lived in the slums, we just got credit for it. The white person is in the ghetto too, but I can't feel sorry for him. He can get out . . . some way. He can change his name to escape racial prejudice, but what can the Negro do? He cannot change anything. He can only sit there . . . trapped.

The white person has the opportunity to better himself, to educate himself, to get a good job, to acquire a loan to buy a house. The Negro has difficulty doing any of these things. And so this is the way it was for me when I was a kid, and if I had not discovered sports, I might still be trapped in the ghetto.

I escaped, and I owe it all to that wonderful woman who was the head of our household and the sole support of seven vigorous, energetic, rapidly growing kids. I must admit I was Mom's favorite, probably because I was her baby and had more than my share of illness when I was little.

I have heard the story so often I sometimes think I actually remember it happening. I couldn't remember it because I was only three and a half at the time. I was seriously ill with pneumonia and Mom had wrapped me in a blanket and my big brother Josh had picked me up in his arms and was carrying me to the hospital. Josh says I looked at him through a pair of big sad eyes and asked, "Am I going to die, Josh?"

"No, Robert," he answered. "You're not going to die. And when you're well, I'm going to buy you a ball and a glove."

My mom has always been in my corner. She always encouraged me in sports and she took time out whenever she could to come and watch me play. Because of her job in the laundry, she didn't have the time other mothers did, but somehow she found the time to watch me play ball. I took it for granted then, but now I realize the sacrifices she made for me in those difficult days.

When I entered high school, she encouraged me to play ball. We needed the money, but she never insisted I go out and work, and if I wanted to play basketball she saw to it that I played. I needed basketball shoes, and she got them for me. I don't know where she got the money, but she got it.

I suppose by all accepted standards we were poor, only we never thought of ourselves as poor. We were a happy family, very close to each other.

How do you measure poverty? I wore the same coat for three or four years. It was a hand-me-down from one of my brothers and I wore it until it had too many holes in it. I had one pair of shoes. No Sunday shoes, just one pair for every day in the week, and I wore them until they practically fell off my feet. When they got holes in the bottom, I put a piece of cardboard in them so the water would not seep through when it rained.

We always had food. Maybe we didn't eat good, but we ate. After Mom went to work in the morning, we would have to get ourselves ready for school. The only milk I remember having was evaporated milk and we added water to it to pour over our cereal.

Christmas in our house was something special. It meant presents. Not toys, usually something we needed. If I needed a pair of shoes, I got a pair of shoes. If I needed a jacket, I got a jacket. When you're a kid and you get a present it's always something great and you are never aware that other kids are getting three times as much.

One Christmas I got a truck. It was a red truck and it had only three wheels and I couldn't understand why one wheel was missing, but I loved that little red truck with three wheels more than anything else in the world. It was something special and I took it with me everywhere I went. I even took it to bed with me. It was Christmas and I had a present and I was happy. Maybe Mom needed a new dress or a new pair of shoes, but she would get by with her old dress and her old pair of shoes so that she could give us Christmas presents. She always made sure we had something . . . even if it was only a little red truck with one wheel missing.

CHAPTER 2 *JOSH*

Growing up without a father is a hardship and a deprivation that is impossible to measure. How can you miss what you never had? How do I know what I missed? I never knew my father. I don't know what kind of man he was. I have no way of telling how my life would have changed had he lived.

In one respect I was fortunate. I had Josh. He was the father I didn't have; the counselor I needed; the companion I wanted; the coach I could not have done without.

Josh was the oldest of us seven kids, fifteen years older than me, the youngest. His real name is LeRoy, but everybody called him Josh. There was a great catcher named Josh Gibson who played in the Negro baseball leagues about that time, but he was not related to us. A lot of people think that is how my brother got his nickname, but I doubt it. The kids in the ghetto never paid much attention to professional sports in those days.

When I was six Josh went off to the army and the only thing I remember about him before he left is that he loved french fried potatoes and ginger ale. He used to go out to the movies and I'd almost die with impatience waiting for him to come home because I knew that meant french fries and ginger ale. I just loved them. I still do.

My recollections of Josh after he came back from the army

11

are vivid. Painfully so. Everytime I look in the mirror I see the scar over my left eye and I am reminded of my big brother.

After his discharge Josh took a job at the packing house. It was the only job he could get. He tried to get a job as a high school teacher, to teach and coach, but he couldn't. He had a master's degree in history but he had to work in the packing house, and I knew that a white person with his qualifications could get a job paying a lot more money.

Josh loved kids and he loved sports, and he wanted to coach so badly he worked at the YMCA coaching basketball and baseball. He got me started in sports with organized teams. The first time I remember playing was with the Urban League. The first organized team I played with was the Y Comets. That was basketball. In baseball I used to play for a man named Red Brummer, who coached midget-league teams in Woodbine, Iowa, which is about 45 miles from Omaha. Red also helped make a ballplayer out of me.

When I was eleven or twelve Josh began to work with me and, because I was his brother, he worked me harder than the rest of the kids. He kept saying that the most important thing in a sport is the fundamentals, so he kept pounding them into me and the rest of the kids in the neighborhood. Fundamentals. Fundamentals. Fundamentals. He talked to us again and again and got us thinking about certain baseball situations till it got so we could do them instinctively.

I always thought he was picking on me because he worked me harder than the rest. I resented it. I got sick and tired of the way he pushed me, and the way he would hit the ball harder at me than he would to anyone else, and make me run longer than anyone else.

Once he hit a ground ball that hit a rock and jumped up and cracked me above the eye and split it open. He stuck a bandaid on it and shoved me back out there, but I ran off the field and went crying to the one person I knew would give me sympathy.

Josh is in the center between me and Buddy Young, the football great.   *OMAHA WORLD-HERALD*

"Robert, don't play with him anymore," Mom said. "Go play with someone else."

"Josh, you leave my baby alone. He's tired. If he don't want to play, he don't have to."

Mom could never understand why I always went back the next day.

I still have the scar over my eye. It is a small price to pay for the other things I took away from those long, tiresome, grueling sessions with Josh. He was great. I didn't know it then, but now as I look back I realize he had my best interests at heart. Pushing me was the best thing he could have done for me, and I appreciate now what I was too young to appreciate then.

Josh was the most influential person in my life as far as my becoming an athlete. And probably a lot of the morals and values and a lot of my thoughts are a direct result of his teaching and training, just as a father would transmit those things to his son.

I was not the only kid in our neighborhood who benefited from Josh's training and teaching, there were hundreds who came under his influence. One was Bob Boozer, star of the Chicago Bulls of the National Basketball Association. At a dinner in Omaha last winter, Bob made a speech and said he probably would not be where he is now if it had not been for Josh. Another athlete who came under Josh's influence is Gale Sayers, the great running back of the Chicago Bears.

Josh was not only my big brother, he was big brother to many kids who needed guidance and someone to take an interest in them at the most difficult time of their lives. Josh gave them what they needed. Every kid should have a big brother like Josh.

CHAPTER 3 *THE QUOTA IS FILLED*

Josh had worked long and hard, had given of himself in time and trouble in attempting to mold a man and an athlete, and now the time had come for me to show that his efforts were not in vain. High school was the place to try to apply all of my big brother's teachings.

I entered Technical High School a pretty good athlete and somewhat full of myself, but first crack out of the box I was slapped down. Hard. I went out for football as a freshman and was turned down because I was too small.

"Go home and eat some meat and potatoes," the coach said, "and come back again next year."

He had a pretty good case since I stood only 4 feet 10 inches tall and weighed only 90 pounds, but I always felt the least he could have done was watch me play. I could outrun most of the players on his team, something I proved later when I competed on the track team.

I consoled my disappointment by telling myself that basketball and baseball were my games anyway, and I got my revenge on the football coach by refusing to join his team when he extended an invitation some years and several pounds later. It was not out of spite. By then I was doing fairly well in baseball and basketball and Josh advised me to stay clear of foot-

15

ball. I always loved football and I would go out and kick and throw the ball way downfield and the coach tried to get me to put on a uniform. I just laughed. I wanted to play but Josh figured a serious injury might ruin whatever future I had in baseball or basketball and I listened to Josh. I wonder if Jimmy Brown, wherever he was, realized that I was leaving him a clear field.

I made the basketball squad in my junior year, but I received another serious jolt to my young ego when I went out for the baseball team.

For some reason I got mixed up on the dates they were holding baseball tryouts and I showed up a day late. The coach ran me right out of there. He said I was too late for the tryout and if I wanted to play baseball, I should go down and join a sandlot team on the near North Side, the Negro area. I was hurt and I had to wait until school was out before I could play baseball.

Josh was coaching a YMCA team in a summer league and I joined up with them. We were called the Y Monarchs and we won the Nebraska State tournament. It was the first championship team I ever played on.

Ironically, the high school coach had a team in that same league. His team was made up mainly of members of the high school squad and everytime we played them we just beat the stuffings out of them. I loved beating them and I guess I tried a little harder against them. I had incentive because here was the same coach who wouldn't let me play on his team. At the time I didn't know the reason he rejected me, but now I have an idea and I definitely think it was because I was a Negro. I recall now that he had no Negroes on his team, although the school was almost 50 percent Negro.

Such was not the case in basketball, however. In fact, four of the five starters on the team were Negroes and the fifth was Glenn Sullivan, my old friend and running mate from the housing project. Our coach was Neal Mosser, who didn't care

My first baseball championship: State midget title with a YMCA team. I'm third from left, front row.

what color you were as long as you could play basketball. He just wanted to win and he would start his five best players no matter who they were. That was the type of individual he was.

Basketball was my favorite sport in those days and my fondest memories of high school are playing basketball and associating with guys on the team. We had a tremendous team and in 1952, my junior year, we played in the state tournament at the University of Nebraska in Lincoln.

We had the biggest and, we thought, the best team in the state. I was the shortest player on the starting five and I was 6 feet. We had one kid 6–1, another 6–3, and two players 6–6 and our first opponent was a team with no player taller than 5–10. We figured to run right over them, but we came down with a severe case of that common malady known as complacency, the great equalizer in sports.

They pressed us on defense and pulled a slowdown on offense and we simply did not know how to cope with those tactics. For three quarters they kept stealing the ball from us, then stalling, forcing us to panic and get overanxious. We just couldn't put the ball in the hoop. I was the second-highest scorer on the team and the best outside shooter. I usually scored on long one-hand jumpers, and when they played me close I would drive around my opponent and pick up points on layups. But that night I was so tight I couldn't make a basket to save myself. They beat us, 40–39, eliminating us from the tournament. I was so disappointed and ashamed I cried my eyes out in the dressing room after the game. It was the last time I can remember crying.

It's great to be young and to have the resiliency to bounce back so quickly after the greatest disappointment of your life. By the time I entered my senior year the pain of losing out in the state tournament was completely forgotten. This was a new year with new goals to strive for and, hopefully, new rewards to be achieved.

Things began to happen for me in my senior year. I had

We were inter-city champs as freshmen. The little guy at the right end of the first row is me.

grown to 175 pounds and I stood 6 feet tall, almost my full growth, and I was getting a reputation as a pretty fair athlete in several sports. We won the city championship in basketball, but were edged out for the district title and the right to go to Lincoln for the state tournament. The disappointment was not so great this time, primarily because I had a very good season. I made all-city but failed to make all-state, and I considered that a slap in the face. I had set all kinds of records and I had done everything on a basketball court that you could imagine, yet they selected someone else from my district on the all-state team. I couldn't help believing the reason they passed me up was because I was a Negro. This is not sour grapes and neither am I the possessor of a persecution complex. I say this because I believe I deserved a place on the all-state team and the records support that belief.

I went out for track and field too, concentrating on the high jump and broad jump. I set an indoor city record in the high jump with 5–11 and got up as high as 6–1 outdoors. In the broad jump I did 22½ feet. When the coach asked me to run on a relay team in the annual Thomas Jefferson Relays in Council Bluffs, Iowa, for schools from Omaha and Council Bluffs, I agreed. I ran the second leg on the 440 and 880 relays and we won both races. I never raced again. I didn't like running like that. I enjoyed running in baseball and basketball, but just running in a race never interested me.

I finally got to play high school baseball in my senior year. As a result of my play in the summer leagues, I had an offer the year before to sign with the Kansas City Monarchs in the Negro Professional League, which I declined without hesitation. I was only fifteen and naturally I was flattered by the offer, but I never seriously considered accepting it. Jackie Robinson had played with the Monarchs and at one time they were considered the big time for a Negro ballplayer. But this was 1952 and Negroes were beginning to appear in major-league uniforms more frequently, and thanks to Jackie Rob-

I guess the Globetrotter in me came out early.

inson and Branch Rickey and everybody who came after them, the Kansas City Monarchs were no longer the be-all and end-all for a Negro baseball player.

I played third base and caught most of the time in high school, but I pitched occasionally and made the all-city team as a utility player. I didn't care what position they picked me for, so long as I was on the team.

Athletically, my senior year was a success. Graduation came and I accepted my diploma and sat back waiting for the college scholarship offers to pour in. They did not pour in. There wasn't even a slow trickle.

Maybe if I had played in a big Eastern city and received more publicity, I might have had a few offers from the basketball powers who scoured the country for players. All I got were a few invitations from small colleges in Nebraska and from Negro colleges. But I was interested in big-time competition. I had my heart set on Indiana University and my basketball coach, Neal Mosser, sent them a letter in my behalf.

I waited on pins and needles for their reply. Each day I went to see coach Mosser, hoping he would have some news, but each day there was none. Finally a letter came and I nearly jumped out of my skin when he summoned me to his office. Sadly, he handed me the letter. I couldn't believe what I read.

"Your request for an athletic scholarship for Robert Gibson has been denied because we already have filled our quota of Negroes."

Quota of Negroes! That was a new one on me. You can bet I made a careful check of their freshman basketball roster the next year. I was interested in seeing what their "quota of Negroes" was. They had one.

When that letter came I was crushed and frustrated. I didn't know where to turn. I recalled that Runt Marr, who was the St. Louis Cardinal scout in our area, had offered me a minor-league contract and now, with all the doors to college seemingly locked to me, the temptation was strong to call Runt and accept his offer.

"Nothing doing," Josh said. "You're going to go to college."

I said that was fine, I wanted very much to go to college because I knew how important it was, but I couldn't figure out how to get there. I had no money, no job, no scholarship, and no hope of getting one. What's more, time was running out. It was less than two months before the beginning of the fall semester.

Then one day Duce Belford came to see me. He likely just dropped out of heaven to solve my problem. I was at the YMCA with Josh when Duce walked in. He was the athletic director of Creighton University in Omaha and he knew Josh, so I guess Josh must have told him about me because he came to the YMCA and asked me if I wanted to go to Creighton. I said yes, I wanted to go anywhere. He said he could fix it so that I got a scholarship.

I raced right home and told Mom I was going to college. I never saw her so happy in all my life.

CHAPTER 4 *OF BOOKS AND BASKETS*

I went to college on a basketball scholarship and I went to play basketball. Not to study. Not to work. Not to improve my mind. Not to earn a degree. Not to prepare for my future. I went to play basketball. That was the only thing that interested me.

I figured all I had to do was play basketball and play it well and I wouldn't have to worry about classes. Was I wrong!

Creighton is run by the Jesuit fathers, who are dedicated to the old-fashioned idea that the reason for going to college is to study. They stay on your back all the time. It didn't matter if you were a basketball player or not, you had to keep up your grades or else you found yourself out on the street where all your press clippings couldn't help you. I just barely made it through my freshman year. If they had bounced me it would have served me right. I had no one to blame but myself.

I took just enough credits to stay eligible for athletics. I got C's and D's and was in danger of dropping out of school. I would come home at night, throw my books in the corner, and forget about them until the next morning. I was spending a good deal of time with the young lady who was to become Mrs. Robert Gibson.

Charline Johnson was Josh's wife's niece. Josh had married his secretary at the YMCA and Charline often came to visit her aunt, and that's where we met. I was seventeen and she was fifteen at the time. We dated a few times, and by the time I was in college we were going steady.

Basketball got me into college and basketball kept me there, but it took a year before I realized how important it was to keep up with my schoolwork. In my sophomore year I not only made the varsity but was playing first-string. I was the first Negro to play varsity baseball or basketball at Creighton.

I was beginning to enjoy playing so much, I started to bear down on my studies so that I could remain eligible to play. I still spent a lot of time at Charline's house and I worked from midnight to 7 A.M. at a filling station, but I found time to study. My major was sociology. I didn't know what I would do with it after school, but I liked the subject. I still wasn't betting on becoming a professional athlete. My only concern was staying eligible for college basketball, and I began to get B's and C's. I was motivated by basketball.

My most vivid memories of college center around basketball. In my sophomore year Creighton started to go big time, scheduling schools like Seton Hall, Loyola of Chicago, Marquette, and Holy Cross.

The game against Holy Cross stands out because they had a tremendous team and a great player, Tom Heinsohn, who later starred with the Boston Celtics. He was their center, and I remember coming up under the basket one time and he knocked the ball right down my throat. So the next time I came up under the same way and there he was again, waiting for me. I gave him a fake and he went up in the air to block the shot again. But this time I left him on one side of the basket and scooted around to the other side and put in a layup.

That gave me a good deal of satisfaction because he was such a great player. They clobbered us, 97–60. Heinsohn scored 24 points. I scored 20, and I was pleased that I had played such a good game against top-flight competition.

I thought I'd never get to college, but here I am playing freshman basketball at Creighton.

Not all my memories of college basketball are pleasant, however. There was the time we played the University of Tulsa. We went to Oklahoma by train and halfway there, Duce Belford told me I would not be able to stay at the same hotel with the rest of the team. He waited until we were on the train to tell me. He knew that if he told me before we left, I would not have made the trip.

We arrived at the Tulsa station and the guys were all hungry, so we decided to go into a restaurant to eat. I was told I could not eat in the restaurant, but they would serve me in the kitchen.

"I'll go with you," said Glenn Sullivan.

"Oh no," I said, "I'm not going in there. I won't eat, that's all. I'll wait until later and go on the other side of town to eat."

"Then I'll go there with you," Glenn said.

So we did. The two of us waited until everyone else finished eating, then we took the bus to their hotel and the other fellows went in and Glenn and I went to the Negro section to eat. Then Glenn came with me to my private hotel. He wanted to stay with me, but I said it wasn't necessary, so he went back to his hotel.

In baseball I played on the varsity team from the time I was a freshman. I pitched some, but I played the outfield most of the time. I also caught and played third base, and anywhere else I was needed. We played only twelve or thirteen games a year, so I didn't get to pitch much. When I did I racked up a lot of strikeouts. I could always throw hard and I was a little wild and hitters were afraid to dig in up there. They just stood there and kind of waved at the ball.

In my senior year we won the Nebraska College Conference title and I led the conference in hitting. I was the centerfielder and a switch-hitter. I didn't stop switching until I began playing pro ball. In college I batted left-handed mostly because there were more right-handed pitchers than left-handers. I hit a few home runs. I had the power to hit the ball over the fences, when there were fences, but I was more of a line-drive hitter. Most of my power was right-handed but I was batting left-handed most of the time.

Each year my hitting and throwing improved enough so that I could feel myself getting better. By my senior year I thought I was a pretty good ballplayer. I had the idea I wanted to play professional basketball or baseball. I preferred basketball.

I had broken every Creighton scoring record in basketball, which held up until a big strong kid named Paul Silas came along to take my records away from me. After I left, Creighton began to recruit in earnest. Silas, who plays with the St. Louis Hawks, was one of their prize catches. I got a few honorable mentions for all-America and a questionnaire from the Minneapolis Lakers, but that was the last I heard from them. I still believed my future was in basketball. My biggest boost in that direction came after the season ended.

The Harlem Globetrotters came to Omaha to play the College All-Stars. They asked me to play with the All-Stars and I agreed. They wanted me on the squad so they could use my name for publicity purposes in my home town to help build up the gate, a fact that became obvious to me when three quarters of the game went by and I still had not left my seat on the bench.

Late in the third period the crowd began to chant: "We want Gibson, we want Gibson!"

Finally, the coach got the message. He looked at me, annoyed.

"All right, Gibson," he droned. "They want you, so get in there."

I played the entire fourth quarter and scored 15 points and we beat the Globetrotters by 1 point. I know the Trotters are not supposed to lose, but we beat them. We didn't have any great players. The only one with any reputation was Lennie Rosenbluth of North Carolina, who didn't impress me as being an all-America. But we had a lot of hustle and that's

how we beat the Trotters, we outhustled them. I kept stealing the ball and driving in for layups and the crowd cheered wildly.

The Trotters must have liked the way I played because their representative, Parnell Woods, asked me if I wanted to join them for the rest of their tour. I said I couldn't because school was still in session, but that I might be interested in hearing from them after school was out. He promised to contact me then.

A lot happened to me that week. Charline and I were married on Sunday. I played against the Globetrotters and was offered a job with them on Monday. And I played a baseball game on Tuesday.

Soon after school ended a letter came from the Globetrotters. Their offer was $500 a month, and the letter said Abe Saperstein would call me shortly. I knew I would not accept their offer. I was a married man now, and was faced with the responsibility and expense of setting up a home. It was not enough money. Besides, although I preferred basketball, I had high hopes I would get a better offer in baseball. Again I was disappointed.

I had a few baseball offers but nothing like what I expected. A Dodger scout told me, "You're not naive enough to think you can play major-league ball, are you?" The Yankees said I wasn't good enough to play Class-D ball. It didn't exactly do wonders for my confidence, but that, I believe, was their intention. I think they were trying to discourage me from asking for a big bonus. I wasn't discouraged. I was looking for $30,-000. They were signing guys left and right for $35,000 and $40,000, and I wanted some of that green.

Runt Marr of the Cardinals was still interested in me. He took me and my brother Josh to see Bill Bergesch, a big, burly, likable man who was the general manager of the Omaha Cardinals, the St. Louis farm team in the Triple-A American Association.

"Look, Bob," Bergesch said, "nobody's going to give you a big bonus. If they give you more than $4,000, the rules say

The Creighton Bluejays varsity team, 1954–55.

they have to carry you on the major-league roster for two seasons and you just don't have enough experience for any club to take a chance on you like that."

"All right," I said, "if that's how it is, I'll just play basketball."

I was counting on getting an offer to play professional basketball, but that offer never came. Instead I got a call from Abe Saperstein. I told him the $500 was not enough and his counteroffer was $7,000 for the full season. That was much less than I expected, so we reached a compromise. He would pay me $1,000 a month for four months after the baseball season. Then I picked up the telephone and called Bill Bergesch. He had impressed me by being so forthright. I told him I was ready to sign with the Cardinals.

I signed a Triple-A contract for $1,000 in bonus and $3,000 in salary to be spread over the remainder of the 1957 season. With baseball and basketball, I was going to make $8,000 for the year. It was not $30,000, but to a kid out of the ghetto it seemed like a fortune.

They signed me as a pitcher-outfielder. They didn't know what I was and I didn't know either. I had no idea what I was going to do, how I was going to try to make it. I just knew I was going to make it. As an outfielder. As a catcher. As a first baseman. As a pitcher. I would play wherever they wanted me to, but I was going to make it.

CHAPTER 5 *THE PROFESSIONAL*

"Loosen up, Bob. When you're ready, go in and pitch batting practice."

The voice was deep and gruff, but there was warmth and kindess in it. It came from a peppery little man in his late forties. He had a leathery weatherbeaten face that was heavily lined, but when he smiled there was a merry twinkle in his eyes that belied his hard exterior and made you feel a certain trust and faith and confidence in him. Once you knew him, you couldn't help liking him.

He had been a pretty good shortstop in his day until his career was cut short when he was hit in the head with a pitched ball. He almost died from the injury, but he recovered and the Cardinals gave him a job in their organization. He had spent twenty years managing in the minor leagues.

Some people thought he deserved a chance in the major leagues, at least as a coach. Others felt he was more valuable to the organization as a minor-league manager. He had studied for the priesthood before going into baseball and his approach was soft and fatherly. He was an excellent teacher with a world of patience and understanding which made him great with young ballplayers. He was the first manager I ever played for in professional baseball. His name was Johnny Keane.

33

"Do you want me to throw hard?" I asked.

"No," he replied, "just half-speed."

It was my first day as a professional ballplayer. I was an Omaha Cardinal, a little frightened, a little awed, a little nervous, a little bewildered. They still did not know at which position I belonged and they were trying to fit me into the right slot.

I went to the mound to pitch batting practice. To my amazement nobody hit the ball out of the cage. These were professional ballplayers one jump away from the big leagues and nobody hit the ball out of the cage. I wasn't really wild, but they couldn't do anything but hit foul balls.

"Throw some curve balls," Johnny Keane shouted.

I threw sliders. I thought they were curve balls. Nobody had ever shown me how to throw a curve ball. They just kept fouling them off.

The hitters were fussing and fuming and I looked at Keane, leaning on a fungo stick behind the batting cage and peering out at me intently.

"Should I start throwing hard?" I naïvely asked.

"No," he said, laughing that warm infectious laugh of his. "No, that's fine."

From that day on I had a position. I was Bob Gibson, pitcher.

For about a week I just sat around and observed, and there was much to observe. I was seeing professional baseball for the first time in my life. Although we lived in Omaha, I never saw the Omaha Cardinals play, partly because I didn't have the money and partly because I was not interested. I didn't see a minor-league game until I played in the minor leagues and I didn't see a major-league game until I played in the major leagues. Not even on television. In the project only one family owned a television set. They must have been rich. We watched it through their window, but never baseball. Usually we watched cowboy movies or cartoons.

As a kid, if I didn't do it I wasn't interested in it. I didn't know anything about professional baseball, football, or basketball. I never collected those trading cards and stuff. I couldn't afford the bubblegum.

My brother Josh followed major-league baseball in the newspapers and occasionally he would go see the Omaha Cardinals play. He was a Dodger fan for the same reason a lot of Negroes were Dodger fans in those days—because of Jackie Robinson.

One day the St. Louis Cardinals came to town to play an exhibition game. I read about it, but I didn't go to the game. It just didn't interest me. The only name I would have known anyway was Stan Musial, and I didn't know too much about him. I knew he was a major-league ballplayer and a good one, but that's all.

About the only professional sport Negroes were really interested in was boxing, because of Joe Louis. I remember going down to the recreation center with a bunch of kids to listen to the broadcast of his fight with Jersey Joe Walcott. I saw Joe Louis in Omaha when I was a little kid. I don't know why he was there, but I was going into the movies as he was coming out and I saw him.

"I know who you are," I said, "you're Joe Louis."

He just smiled and that was all. He is the only celebrity I can recall seeing when I was little and, frankly, I was more excited about going to the movie than I was about seeing Joe Louis.

Now I was a professional baseball player. At least I was on the roster of a professional baseball team. A week passed and all I did was sit on the bench. Then one night our pitcher was getting bombed and Keane looked down the bench at me.

"OK, Bob," he said. "Go down to the bullpen and warm up."

That was all. No warning, no fanfare, no advance publicity. That was how I made my professional debut. I gulped hard and got up and ran down to the bullpen. I was so excited, I grabbed the wrong glove. Minutes later I was walking into a professional game for the first time.

My mother was in the stands, but I wasn't thinking about her being there. I couldn't think of anything. I was too nervous. My nervousness left me when I started pitching, although I could never prove that by my performance. I walked the first three men I faced.

I wasn't very wild, I was just missing. I kept throwing everything high, across the letters. I thought they were strikes, but the umpire kept shouting "Ball!"

I tried to adjust and got the ball down around the knees. Again the umpire shouted "Ball!"

I guess I panicked because I threw the ball away and the next thing I knew they had three runs and Johnny Keane was coming to the mound. Some debut!

"That's pretty good for a first time," he said softly. "We'll get back to you later."

And that's just the kind of man Johnny was. He would never embarrass a young ballplayer. He would always have a word of encouragement for him.

Things improved somewhat after I got over the initial shock. John worked with me on the sidelines, helping me adjust my stride so that I would get the ball down in the strike zone. He used me quite a bit after that. I appeared in ten games and I won 2 and lost 1. I was showing improvement with each game, and with the improvement came confidence, which is so important for all athletes.

After two months with Omaha, they told me they were sending me down to Columbus, Georgia, which didn't exactly cause me to jump for joy. I was so unhappy about not getting a big bonus to begin with that I made them promise they would not send me any lower than Omaha, but they did anyway. They had signed some hot-shot pitcher from Washington —I don't even remember his name—and they had to make room for him, so I had to go. The last place in the world I wanted to go was Columbus, Georgia.

It was the first time I had ever been in the South. I spent a month there, it only seemed like a year. I thought Columbus was the worst place in the world. Later I found out there are many places just as bad.

One consolation was that I got a chance to pitch more in Columbus that I would have in Omaha. In a month I appeared in eight games, pitching 43 innings. I won 4 and lost 3 and my control improved a little.

Finally, the season ended. In three months I had won 6 and lost 4. Not bad for a starter, I thought. I went home and prepared to join the Harlem Globetrotters.

There were, in reality, two Harlem Globetrotters, one team in the East, another in the West. I started with the East and midway I switched to the West. I was the new kid on the block and the veteran players treated me accordingly. I don't mean they snubbed me or were discourteous to me in any way. Just that they made me know my place. They kept reminding me of my lowly status. They rarely called me by name. It was always "Hey, rook." I had to sit in the back of the bus right over the wheel. We would drive all night and most of the players slept on the bus, but I could never fall asleep. I tossed and turned and waited until we got where we were going before I could get any sleep.

When I read stories about my days with the Globetrotters, they usually make me out to be a star. I wasn't a star on the Trotters, I was just another player. I played with guys like Tex Harris, Bobby Milton, J. C. Gibson and Meadowlark Lemon. Can you imagine me being a star on a team with Meadowlark Lemon? Some chance.

The way it works with the Globies, the center is always the star. He does most of the clowning. Everybody else works off him. The rest of the players do a three-man or four-man figure 8 around the center. Everybody clowns once in a while.

If you're going to play with the Harlem Globetrotters you're going to have to clown sometimes. It didn't have to be anything special. You did whatever you could do. Usually you just improvised. Whatever came to you at that moment, that's what you did. There were specialists, of course. They tried to make me into a dribbling expert, but I didn't want any part of it.

I played quite a bit with the Globetrotters. I guess you could say I was a regular because I was always in the pregame circle and since I was the shortest player on the team at 6–1, I would go in and dunk the ball after we got through with our customary clowning.

We practiced for three weeks before the season opened, going over routines, old and new. Once the season started we never practiced again. There was no time to practice. We were playing almost every night and when we weren't playing we were traveling. We really didn't have to practice. After you did a routine once or twice you knew pretty much what was going to happen and you fell right in step with it.

We did have a pattern. For instance, with a minute left in the first quarter we did one thing. Then maybe at the start of the fourth quarter we did something else. The rest of the clowning was just spontaneous, nothing that we had a script for. Usually it involved ball-handling. That was one thing the Globetrotters made sure of before they signed you, that you could handle the ball.

I never went too much for the clowning. I enjoy playing basketball, period, and I always enjoyed the second and third periods most because that was when we usually played it straight. I was more amused than amusing. I knew pretty quick that I didn't want to make a career out of playing with the Harlem Globetrotters.

I knew it, but I didn't let Bing Devine know it. Bing was the general manager of the St. Louis Cardinals. He was an old basketball player himself, but he wasn't too crazy with the idea that I was playing with the Globetrotters during the off-season. He called me and told me so.

This gave me my chance to become a Globetrotter. Our college All-Stars beat the Trotters.

I told him it really wasn't dangerous or anything and that I was making pretty good money playing with them. It was sort of an off-season job and I needed the money because Charline was about to have a baby.

"Bob," he said, "I really don't think you can concentrate on both sports and give them both your best."

He was right, of course, and when he asked me to quit basketball I said I would—after he said the Cardinals would make up the money I would lose by not playing with the Globetrotters.

I hope that clears up another misconception. It has been written that the reason I quit the Globetrotters was because my asthma was acting up. That is not the truth. I haven't had an asthma attack since I was a little boy. I guess that story came from my mother. Everytime a reporter talks to her she tells him about me almost dying when I was little and that I have a heart murmur and about one side of my chest being lower than the other and all the rest. Once and for all, I did not quit the Globetrotters because of asthma. I quit because Bing Devine asked me to, but I did not quit until he agreed to make it worth my while to do so.

Actually, I was feeling pretty good about Devine taking such an interest in me. I had been in the organization less than one season and he had taken the trouble to contact me and ask me to give up basketball. I figured they must have had high hopes for me. I could hardly wait to get going in 1958.

CHAPTER 6 *NO ROOM AT THE INN*

The letter arrived early in January. It was from the St. Louis Cardinals. I tore it open excitedly and read:

"The St. Louis Cardinals invite you to train with them in St. Petersburg, Florida. The players will be staying at the Bainbridge Hotel. Pitchers and catchers are to report in uniform at Al Lang Field on February 8."

This was my big chance. I had less than a year's experience in professional baseball and I was being given an opportunity to train with the big team. If I could make a good impression down there I might be in the major leagues long before I had planned.

I waited impatiently for the time to pass so that I could get going. Finally, it came and I left Charline and the baby, little Renee, in Omaha and took a train to Florida. The trip from Omaha to St. Petersburg took a couple of days, but I passed the time thinking about my future as a member of the St. Louis Cardinals. When I arrived in St. Pete, I jumped in a cab and instructed the driver to take me to the Bainbridge Hotel. I thought nothing of it when he gave me a kind of strange look.

We arrived at the hotel, pulling up in an alley in front of a side door. I went to the desk and got that same strange look from the clerk.

"My name is Bob Gibson," I announced proudly. "I'm with the St. Louis Cardinal ball club. You're supposed to have a place for me."

He looked at a piece of paper and gave the cabdriver an address. The cabbie hustled me back out the side door and back into his cab. I was beginning to get the message loud and clear.

We drove across the railroad tracks to the other side of town. I didn't have to see the people in the street to know we were in the Negro district. We pulled up to a private house. There were six or seven other Negro ballplayers there, including Curt Flood and Sad Sam Jones. They weren't the only Negro players in the Cardinal camp that year; they were simply all that could be accommodated in this particular house. The others lived in other houses with Negro families.

The house where we lived was owned by a woman who charged us each $49 a week for a room and a couple of meals a day. It was a shame . . . and a terrible disappointment. I had traveled more than 2,000 miles and I still had not escaped the ghetto. "So this," I said to myself, "is the major leagues."

Three years later the club had moved its spring-training headquarters and I was welcome at the new hotel. I took this opportunity to give my wife and daughters a Florida vacation. It was a decision I was to regret.

We drove from Omaha to St. Petersburg, but everything in between was disgusting and degrading. We could not eat because most of the restaurants would not serve us. We could not stop for the night when we were tired because most of the motels would not accommodate us.

When we were hungry or tired, we drove—sometimes for miles—to the Negro section of town where we would be put up for the night or where we could buy some sandwiches, which we ate in the car.

One time we stopped at a filling station for gas. The attendant, a white Southern "gentleman," had no objection to selling me gasoline. But when I asked if my girls might use the ladies' room, he directed them to a room in the back of the station. The sign above the door said *Colored Only*. Angry and humiliated, I told him, "Forget the gas," and drove off.

Back in that first spring-training camp in 1958, I was mostly concerned with making a good showing. But I lasted in camp just two weeks, hardly time enough to learn the way to the ballpark, then they sent me to the minor-league training center in Daytona Beach. I guess I was a little cocky in those days. I had so much confidence in myself, I felt I could pitch in the majors if given the chance, and when they sent me away I was hurt. I'm sure Fred Hutchinson, the manager, never even noticed me. There were so many young ballplayers swarming around the field, I would have had to stand on my head to be noticed . . . or at least strike out Stan Musial four times in a row. That was impossible. I wasn't there long enough to see Musial, or anybody else, for that matter.

They assigned me to Omaha, which took some of the sting out of my disappointment. I was back in my home town, back with Johnny Keane, a manager I knew and liked and one who knew and, I think, liked me. Most important, I was thankful that they were not asking me to serve another sentence in Columbus, Georgia.

Keane brought me along slowly. After thirteen games I had a record of 3–4, but more important than that was my earned-run average and my strikeout-walk ratio. In my first year, my ERA was 4.29 at Omaha and 3.77 at Columbus. And, at both places, I walked more men than I struck out. This time I got my ERA down to 3.31 and struck out 47 men in 87 innings, while walking only 39.

For this I was sent to Rochester in the International League. It was considered a promotion . . . by everyone but me. I was not too anxious to leave home, nor was I happy about leaving

Keane and coming under a new manager who might not be as sympathetic and considerate as John. But I was getting paid to play ball and when the boss says "Go" you go.

At Rochester my manager was Cot Deal. He didn't use me much at first, but I got along with him fine. Fortunately for me, another pitcher, Lyn Lovenguth, did not get along with him. Shortly after I arrived, Lyn started a game and got in trouble in the first inning. Deal went to the mound to talk to him. The next thing I knew, they were going after each other pretty good. Cot was chewing Lovenguth out and Lyn was giving it right back to him. Finally, the pitcher stormed off the mound, went to the clubhouse, changed into his street clothes, packed a bag, and went home.

Cot sent me into the game to replace Lovenguth. I pitched a shutout the rest of the way and from then on, I took Lovenguth's place in the starting rotation. Thank you, Lyn Lovenguth, wherever you are!

At Rochester for the last two months, I won 5 games and lost 5. My earned-run average was a respectable 2.45. My walks vs. strikeouts were even better than at Omaha—75 strikeouts, 54 walks in 103 innings.

Once again, in the spring of 1959, the Cardinals invited me to train with them in St. Petersburg. This time I stayed longer. Long enough for somebody to hang the nickname "Hoot" on me, after Hoot Gibson, the old movie cowboy. And long enough for me to meet Stan Musial.

I found Stan to be a friendly, talkative guy. When you're young you have the feeling the older ballplayers kind of look down on you a little, that you have to break the barrier in some way to become one of the guys. Musial was not at all like that. He was the same with everybody, whether you were a rookie or a ten-year veteran. He used to sit down and talk to me a lot. Not about anything in particular, just small talk, and he wasn't going out of his way to be especially nice to me. He talked with everyone, that's the kind of guy he is.

I posed for this in my first spring training with the Cardinals, but I had little reason to smile.

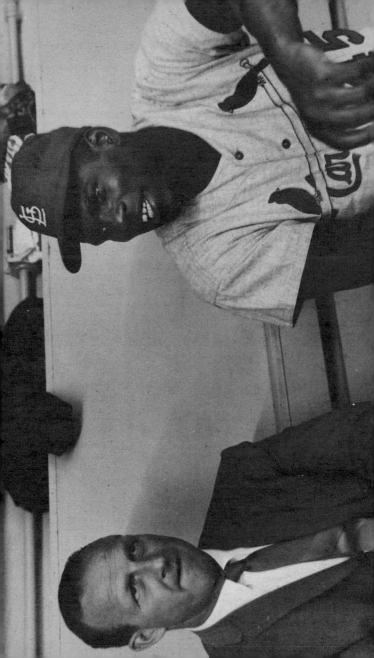

One day I was sitting in the dugout in Al Lang Field and Musial was standing alongside me. "See that light tower up there?" he said, pointing at a tower high on top of the stands over 400 feet away in right-center field.

"Yeah," I said, "I see it."

"One day I hit a ball over that thing." And he just laughed real hard and walked away and I know he wasn't boasting or anything. It was just the way he was, friendly and talkative. Later, when I became his teammate, people always asked me what kind of person Stan Musial was. Was he a good guy to have on a ball club? I would say he was a nice, friendly person. He wasn't a rah-rah, team-spirit kind of guy, but he was a good guy to have on a ball club. Anybody who could hit like he did is good to have on a ball club.

I survived spring training and started the 1959 season with the Cardinals, but I was soon sent back to Omaha. Johnny Keane had finally been given a major-league job, as a Cardinal coach. Joe Schultz had replaced him at Omaha. By now I was considered a good prospect and the Cardinals sent me down and instructed Schultz to use me in the regular starting rotation. I pitched in 24 games, completed 10 and had a record of 9–9. My earned-run average was 3.07, not bad. I struck out 98 and walked only 46 in 135 innings. Pitching regularly, my early wildness practically vanished. That pleased me and evidently it pleased the Cardinals. They brought me back again at the end of the season for another look. My combined record with them for the year was 3–5.

I was sure 1960 was going to be my year, especially when I started the season with the Cardinals. But I was used sparingly and sent to Rochester, where I pitched in six games, completed 3 and won 2 of 5 decisions. Three weeks later I was back in St. Louis to stay. I should have been content. It should have been a dream come true. Instead it was a nightmare, and all because of Solly Hemus.

Solly Hemus had been a run-of-the-mill major-league ball-

I found Stan Musial to be a warm, friendly, talkative guy.
                                                            Ken Regan

player with the Cardinals and Phillies in the 1950's. He was
short on playing talent, but long on hustle, guts, and desire.
He was a battler. He did everything he could to make himself
into a valuable ballplayer despite his limited ability and for
that he deserves all the credit in the world. I will never downgrade a man professionally regardless of what I might think
about him personally.

In 1956, the Cardinals had traded Hemus to Philadelphia
and Solly wrote a letter to Mr. August Busch, president of
the St. Louis ball club. He told him what a pleasure it was
playing with such an outstanding organization as St. Louis
and how happy he was to have been a part of that organization. Mr. Busch never forgot that letter. He remembered it
when he was searching for a manager in 1959 and he got
Hemus back from the Phillies and made him manager of his
club.

Hemus managed like he played—with a chip on his shoulder. He did everything he could think of to win and when he
did not win he blamed everybody except himself.

For some reason he didn't care for me. I guess it must have
been a personality clash more than anything else, but he never
did like me and he rarely used me. I was so bored I would sit
on the bench in the far corner of the dugout and I'd just about
fall asleep because it's no fun when you're not playing. Musial
used to walk over to me all the time, nudge me and say, "Hey,
wake up, it's time to go home."

The few times I did get a chance to pitch, I could not possibly be sharp because of lack of work. Especially when I
went eight or nine days without pitching. I'd be exceptionally
strong and the ball would move every which way. I never
knew where it was going and, as a result, I walked a lot of
men and made too many mistakes.

The only time I was sure of pitching was when we played
Pittsburgh and Vernon Law was pitching for the Pirates, or
when we played the Milwaukee Braves and Warren Spahn was
scheduled to pitch.

Perhaps I am defeating my argument by admitting I was lousy whenever I got the chance to pitch. True, I was lousy, and based on what I did when I got a chance, maybe I did not deserve to pitch regularly. My point is that nobody can pitch well if he is not used often enough to keep sharp, particularly a young pitcher. Besides, I was not the only player who was held back by Hemus. He had Bill White, the best first baseman in the league, playing center field. And he had Curt Flood, the best centerfielder in the league, sitting on the bench. How he could get a job as a manager, I'll never know.

One rare day I started a game. I walked the first man and the next batter hit a high fly ball to center field. It should have been caught, but Bill White, who didn't belong out there in the first place, misjudged it. The ball came down and nearly hit Bill on the head. It fell behind him and the man on first raced all the way around to score. Out came Hemus, ranting and raving, and signaling to the bullpen for a new pitcher.

"Why are you taking me out?" I asked.

"Get some damn body out and I'll leave you in a ballgame," he raged.

It wasn't only that he didn't use me that made me dislike Hemus. It was the way he treated me, the way he humiliated me in front of the entire ball club. He used to say, "You'll never be a pitcher. All you do is throw, you never pitch."

We'd have a meeting to go over the opposing hitters and he would say, "Gibson, you don't have to pay any attention to this. You just try to get the ball over the plate." That's embarrassing. I had been pitching just a couple of years and that's not exactly encouragement for a young pitcher. I think his biggest problem was that he just used poor psychology more than anything else.

One day I was taking a shower after a game. Ray Sadecki was in there, too. He had just pitched a pretty good game. In came Hemus. "See, Gibson," he said. "That's the way you're supposed to pitch, not just throw like you do." How can you like a guy who says things like that to you over and over?

The club got off badly in 1961. In midseason Solly Hemus was fired and Johnny Keane was named to replace him. I am not going to be a hypocrite and say I was sorry to see Hemus lose his job. And for him to be replaced by the first manager I ever played for, well, that was almost too good to be true. I felt as if I had been let out of jail. The day it happened, Keane came over to me and handed me the ball. "You're pitching tonight, Hoot," he said softly. "And from now on you're in the regular rotation."

I'll never forget that day. The date was July 6. Independence Day came two days late that year.

CHAPTER *7* *MAKING IT*

At bat was Mel Queen of the Cincinnati Reds, a young left-handed hitter, but one who had not played very much. I had nursed a 1-run lead into the ninth inning. I retired the first two batters and jumped ahead of Queen, a pinch-hitter, no balls, two strikes. I figured I could get him with a hard slider on the inside part of the plate.

I wouldn't even have to get it in the strike zone, just close enough. If he didn't swing, chances are the umpire would call it a strike anyway. But if I got it that close, Queen would have to swing. It would be a tough pitch to hit. He could not possibly hit it good and keep it in fair territory.

I was ready. I pumped into my motion, my arms swinging freely and vigorously. I rocked back on my right leg and kicked my left leg high. Pivoting on my right foot and using my hips as a swivel to bring my body around, my right arm was a catapult as it rocketed the ball toward home plate with all the force and power I could muster.

Oh, oh! I did not get the ball where I wanted it. I missed my spot by no more than an inch and a half. I got it too far out over the plate. I knew before he hit it that it was a bad pitch, and when Queen jumped at it, everyone else in the ballpark knew it too.

You could tell by the crack of the bat where it was going. I did not even turn around to look. I didn't have to. I knew where it was going. Right over the fence. Tie score. I picked up the resin bag and slammed it down on the mound in disgust. I pounded my fist angrily into the pocket of my glove. I was mad. Not at Mel Queen. Not at the resin bag. Not at my glove. I was made at myself. I had made a mistake.

I retired the side and walked off the mound, kicking and stomping, so angry with myself I could hardly see straight. I noticed Johnny Keane out of the corner of my eye. His hands were jammed into the back pockets of his uniform trousers. His face was red with anger. He was fuming.

I tried to pass by him without looking his way. He wouldn't let me. He jumped right down my throat. "What kind of pitch was that, Hoot?" he growled. "How could you throw him a pitch he could hit out in a situation like that? Why don't you think out there?"

That did it. I saw red. Not that bit again, I said to myself. Solly Hemus had been gone two years. I thought I had heard the last of that kind of stuff. I jumped right back at Keane.

"Dammit, John," I shouted, "I was thinking. I had something in mind. I just didn't get the ball where I wanted it."

Most people, managers and players included, think when you get 0–2 on a batter you have to waste a pitch or two to set him up. I just cannot see that. What are you accomplishing if you throw the ball a foot over a batter's head? What are you setting him up for when you do that? He's not going to swing at it. He's just going to stand there and watch it go by and all you have done is waste a pitch.

When I get 0–2 on a hitter I like to get him out with that next pitch. I throw a lot of pitches as it is, I don't need to throw any extra ones. I don't care anything about strikeouts. If I get two strikes on a batter I'll try to strike him out, but I'd much rather get him on the first pitch, because that's going to cut down the amount of pitches I throw in a game and I might not get as tired.

In my early days as a Cardinal, when I let the ball go, I was never sure exactly where it would go.   *UPI*

When I have games in which I don't strike out many batters the reporters come to me and say, "You weren't throwing good. You didn't strike out many guys."

"So what," I tell them. "I won, didn't I? That's the main thing."

I guess it's because they associate the kind of stuff I throw with a lot of strikeouts. Believe me, I would much rather get three outs on three pitches than three outs on nine pitches, because that's going to make me that much stronger at the end of the game.

My pitching philosophy is simple. I believe in getting the ball over the plate and not walking a lot of men. I don't believe in wasting a pitch. An 0–2 pitch, I think, should be inviting enough for the batter to swing at, but not good enough for him to hit out. I think you've got to make it close enough to the strike zone so the batter might swing at it or the umpire might call it a strike. But no pitcher can get every pitch exactly where he wants it every time. That's why batters hit home runs. If a pitcher always got the ball where he wanted it, no batter would ever get a hit off him.

And that's just what happened to me against Mel Queen. Keane got mad at me because he thought it was carelessness. He wanted me to do some thinking. I got mad at him because I *was* thinking.

John was normally an easy-going guy, but he had his occasional bursts of temper. This was the second time he had jumped at me. I was disappointed in him because I thought it would have been in better taste to wait until we were alone before he said something—as he usually did—and because I thought I had convinced him I did not pitch without thinking. I would have expected that from Solly Hemus, not from Johnny Keane. I realized, however, that there was a great deal of strain on him. We had started out slowly that year, 1963, and he was under pressure to win and in danger of losing his job. I tried to forget the incident and hoped I convinced him I knew what I was doing on the mound.

Things had changed dramatically for me after Keane took over as manager in the middle of the 1961 season. That was my first big break. If there is any individual who gave me the confidence in my ability to be a major-league pitcher, it was Johnny Keane. From July 6, when he replaced Hemus, until the end of the season, I won 11 games and lost 6, finishing with a record of 13–12. My earned-run average of 3.24 was the fifth best in the league and the best among right-handed pitchers. I struck out 166 and walked 119 in 211 innings. I led the league in walks, but most of them came in the first half of the season when I wasn't pitching regularly.

We finished the 1961 season in a tie for fifth place. The following year we slipped to sixth. I won 15, more than any other Cardinal pitcher, and lost 13, and my ERA improved to 2.85. For the first time I struck out over 200 batters, 208 to be exact, in 234 innings and I made the All-Star team. Pitching regularly meant all the difference.

I might have won one or two more games in 1962, but with about a week left in the season I broke a bone in my right ankle when my spikes caught in the dirt as I was taking batting practice. I spent most of the winter in a cast and the ankle was still a little weak when the 1963 season started. As a result, I got off to a very slow start. So did the Cardinals.

By then I had become firmly established in the Cardinal rotation and things were looking up. In addition to better control as a result of regular work, two things contributed to my improvement. I added a curve ball to my repertoire and I discovered I could throw two kinds of fast balls.

In the spring of 1959, Howard Pollet, the Cardinal pitching coach who had been an outstanding left-handed pitcher for the Cardinals after World War II, was working with me one day. He asked me to throw a curve ball, which I did . . .

or thought I did. What I thought was a curve ball was a hard, fast, flat curve . . . a slider. Howie taught me how to throw a curve ball properly, to roll my wrist and dig down on the ball so that it drops down when it reaches the plate. A curve ball is not something you can pick up overnight. It took me years to perfect mine. At first I kept bouncing it in the dirt and I never threw it in a game. I would work on the curve ball on the sidelines. Whenever I played catch with somebody, I would throw curve balls until I could control it enough to try it in a game.

Ordinarily you don't find a pitcher who has a real good curve ball and a good slider. He either has one or the other. One exception is Juan Marichal. Sandy Koufax, for instance, never threw a slider.

As a pitcher gets older his slider usually becomes less effective. That's because a slider must be thrown hard to be effective and as you lose some zip off the ball, the slider loses its effectiveness. A curve ball is not thrown as hard as the slider to begin with, so when a pitcher loses some of his zip, he will usually go to the curve ball more often.

Curve balls are more effective in the early part of a game. In the late innings, when you are a little tired, you cannot dig down on the curve ball and it has a tendency to hang, and hanging curves are hit over fences. I try to stick with fast balls and sliders late in a game. You can get by with that hard stuff if you make a mistake. You can't with a curve ball because it's rolling slowly and the batter can see it a lot longer than a fast ball or slider, and that extra split second gives him time to adjust and whack it.

Late in the game, even if you are not throwing as hard as you did earlier, you can be a little off and still get by with the fast ball or slider because the ball moves more when you're tired. But I'd rather throw hard and not have it move quite as much than to be tired and have it move but not be able to hit those spots. If you are hitting those spots when you're tired, you're going to be all right. If you're not throwing the ball where you want it, you're going to get killed no matter how much your ball is moving.

I discovered, by fooling around on the sidelines in 1961, that I could make my fast ball do different things depending on how I held it. When I held it across the seams, as I always did, the ball sailed away from a right-handed hitter. When I held it with the seams, I found that the ball would sink and tail into a right-handed hitter. I discovered this quite by accident. You're always messing around, trying to figure out what you can do with a pitch or how the ball will react to a certain way you hold it.

So I had two fast balls. One—the sailer—is my "out" pitch, the one I get most of my strikeouts with. The other—the sinker—I use when the situation calls for a double-play ball. They will usually beat the sinker into the ground. Having two fast balls doesn't make me unique or anything. A lot of pitchers can make the ball move two different ways.

To throw my fast ball that sails I hold the ball across the seams. All my other pitches I throw with the seams. On the sinking fast ball, I try to turn the ball over—that is, twist my wrist counterclockwise as I release it. I like to throw the sinker to left-handed hitters because it is moving away from them, but I cannot control it as well as I can my sailer. I can get it down, but I cannot get it in and out the way I would like to. Consequently, I throw the sailing fast ball more frequently than the sinker.

The curve ball is thrown with a big roll of the wrist, which accounts for the big downward break and the slowness of the ball. With the slider I try to cut through the ball with my fingers, and with a stiff wrist.

I went into the 1963 season armed with four pitches—two fast balls, a curve ball, and a slider. I also throw a changeup, but only on rare occasions. The variety helped me become a better pitcher.

Because of the tenderness that remained in my ankle after the break, I labored through the first month of the season. When my ankle got stronger, my pitching improved.

By midseason we were somewhere in the middle of the standings, pretty far behind the pace-setting Los Angeles Dodgers. Then, in mid-August, we caught fire. We won nineteen out of twenty games and the Dodgers came in to play a three-game series in St. Louis late in the season. They led us by two games. If we swept all three we would take over first place. If we won two out of three, we would trail by only one game. We felt certain we would overtake them. We had momentum going for us and the advantage of our home grounds.

It was not to be. Johnny Podres beat Ernie Broglio, 3–1, in the first game. In the second game, Sandy Koufax pitched a four-hitter and beat Curt Simmons, 4–0. Suddenly momentum had swung to their side as we prepared to play the last game of the series. We were four games behind and time was running out. It was my turn to pitch the third game. We had expected to face Don Drysdale, but Dodger manager Walt Alston went to a young lefthander, Pete Richert, because the Dodgers had won the first two games with lefthanders. If I could win, it would leave us three behind with seven games still to be played—time enough to catch them.

We got rid of Richert in three innings and held a 5–1 lead going into the eighth. I had allowed only four hits to that point, but suddenly I lost my stuff. Three singles and a walk made it 5–2 and Keane took me out of the game. I hated to leave. I was sure I could hold them, but John wanted a fresh pitcher, Bobby Shantz.

Bobby had no better luck and he needed help from Ron Taylor to get out of the inning. We still had a 1-run lead going into the ninth, but a kid named Dick Nen spoiled it all for us.

Nen was playing in his first major-league game. He had been called up from Spokane that day and arrived at the ball park after the game had started. Nobody on our club knew anything about him. We had not even covered him in our pregame meeting. When he was announced as a pinch-hitter in the eighth, we all turned to each other and said, "Dick who?"

We found out who "Dick who?" was an inning later. He flied out the first time, but Alston left him in the game to play first base and he came to bat with one out in the ninth and hit the ball on the roof to tie the game. The Dodgers finally won it in the thirteenth. It was a great run while it lasted, but the Cardinals were finished for 1963.

All in all it had not been a bad year even if it did come to a disappointing conclusion. I won 18 games and lost 9. Our late spurt saved Johnny Keane's job and we picked up second-place money. It gave us good reason to look forward with hope and confidence to 1964.

CHAPTER 8 *FIFI*

Fifi LaTour was in a slump. The "grand old lady of burlesque" was doing almost as badly as the St. Louis Cardinals. In the spring, Fifi predicted the Cardinals would win the 1964 National League pennant. Not only that, she predicted we would finish with a .590 percentage.

We never saw Fifi. Her predictions came in the form of letters—about one a week—which were immediately tacked up on the bulletin board for all to see. It was funny that Fifi's handwriting was curiously similar to that of Doc Bauman, our trainer.

Now Fifi LaTour was in a slump. On July 9, two days after the All-Star game, we lost to the New York Mets, 4–3, in the ninth inning. It put us in sixth place, eleven games off the pace of the runaway Philadelphia Phillies and two games under .500 with a 39–41 record.

After our spectacular finish in 1963, a lot of people—including Fifi LaTour—predicted we would win the 1964 pennant. We had a basically sound ball club, but we got off to a bad start and just couldn't get going and a lot of people—including Fifi LaTour—were asking, "What's wrong with the Cardinals?"

"I'm what's wrong with the Cardinals," Bill White, our first baseman and leading hitter, said to a reporter. "I've got only 30 runs batted in. I should have twice that many. I've got to start hitting."

In a way Bill was right. He was off to a terrible start and we did need his bat. He had knocked in 100 or more runs and hit 20 or more home runs for the previous three seasons and we looked to him and Kenny Boyer to supply the power for us. When you're losing, everybody feels he should be doing more to help the team, but Bill wasn't the only one who was playing far below his potential. Most of us were, myself included.

By the All-Star break I had won only 5 games and lost 6. Bing Devine, our general manager, called me into his office. "Let's forget what has passed, Bob," he said. "If you can win 10 games the second half of the season, I'll treat it as if you have won 20 at contract time."

That certainly was fair and gave me incentive, if incentive was what I needed. It wasn't. What I needed was runs. After winning my first 4 games, I lost my next 4 when we scored a total of 3 runs.

Still, that was no excuse. I should have had more than 5 victories and I knew it better than anybody. We all knew we should have been doing more. We even had a few meetings without the manager to try and kick ourselves in the butt and play a little harder and do something. Bill White and Dick Groat kind of took command of the meetings, but we all had something to say. We just talked over our problems and what was wrong and what we wanted to try to do. We had to hustle more, run more, be more daring on the bases.

The meetings always helped us—for a little while. We would put together a streak of 4 or 5 victories, then we would lose 2 or 3 in a row and be right back where we started.

On August 23, we lost to San Francisco, 3–2. We were in fourth place, eleven games behind the Phillies with only 39 games left. Looking at it that way, in cold, hard figures, it seemed an impossible task. But things can happen—and they did.

It is difficult to pinpoint the turning point in the season for us. Most likely it came way back on June 15, the trading deadline, but none of us realized it at the time. Bing Devine made the trade that would prove to be the turning point for us. He sent Ernie Broglio to the Chicago Cubs in return for Lou Brock. It didn't exactly shake up the baseball world when it happened.

Left field had been the one trouble spot in our lineup. Stan Musial had retired after the 1963 season and we could not find a replacement for him. Four or five guys had a shot at it, but nobody could do it until Brock came along.

I remember telling a reporter that I didn't think too much of the trade, and I didn't. Ernie had won 18 games for us the year before. He was a good veteran pitcher and the one thing we could least afford to give up, it seemed to me, was pitching. Particularly for a player like Brock, who was hitting something like .250 for the Cubs. I wondered if we got enough in return for Broglio.

Looking back, I can recall that when Brock was with the Cubs, somebody on our team said the way he can run, Lou would probably lead the league in hitting one day. I was doubtful. He never impressed me like that. The few times I pitched against him I never had any trouble with him. To me he was just another outfielder.

I am happy to say I was wrong. It took him about six weeks to get going, but when he did he really picked the club up. He was the missing link in our offense. Batting first, he always seemed to be on base when the big hitters came up. He began stealing bases and taking the extra base and upsetting the other teams with his speed and daring on the bases.

A thing like this happens slowly, almost without warning. You win a couple of games and the team ahead of you loses a couple and just like that you are closing in on them. You begin to get the big hit at the right time, you win a few games with late-inning rallies, the pitching tightens up. If you score 1 run, the opposition scores none. If you give up 5, your team gets you 6. Suddenly you have momentum and the belief that you might not lose another game.

Just about that time we got another letter from "Fifi." She predicted the Phillies would go into a decline and we would come on and win the pennant and that Sadecki would win a World Series game in St. Louis and I would win one in New York.

We tried to look at things more objectively, to evaluate our chances of overtaking the Phillies. We knew we had an outside chance, but everything had to go right for us and wrong for them. You hope for a thing like that to happen, but you don't expect it will.

Curt Simmons and I had several conversations during which we tried to draw a comparison between our club and Philadelphia's. Naturally, you always think your club is the best club. Every day you go out to play you are confident you are going to win. That's the only way to be. So we thought we had the better club. We knew we lacked power. We had only two guys who could hit home runs—Boyer and White—but we felt we had something else. Curt and I agreed we compensated for it with speed and hustle, and that is why I feel Lou Brock was the difference for us.

You remember what happened. Even as I am retelling it here, it seems impossible to believe. Right after that game in San Francisco, our lowest point in the season, we began to make our move. We won our next 6 games and just like that we had lopped four games off the Phillies' lead and the guys were beginning to get ideas. Fifi LaTour was making a stirring comeback.

We went into Philadelphia on September 9 for a two-game series, trailing by six games. If we could win both, we'd be only four behind. We won the first, 10–5, but Chris Short beat

Ray Sadecki in the second, 5–1, and we were still six games back and time was running out. The Phillies appeared to have locked it up with that game. Our dressing room was a tomb. Our hopes were dashed. Only twenty games remained and, frankly, we were willing to settle for second-place money, which would have represented a pretty good comeback in itself.

It was up to me to pitch the following game against Chicago and try to put us back on the winning track. I beat the Cubs, 5–0, for my fifth-straight victory. It was also my tenth since the All-Star game, the number of victories Bing Devine had asked of me. I could sense that beating the Cubs lifted the club once again.

We beat Chicago 2 out of 3, beat Milwaukee 2 out of 3, but lost 2 out of 3 to Cincinnati. We were on a treadmill, going nowhere. We could not cut into the Phillies' lead, still six games, as we went to New York for a two-game series with twelve games left. Up ahead was an important three-game series against Philadelphia in St. Louis. We hoped we could stay within striking distance so the series would be meaningful. If the Phillies were going to win, let them win it by knocking us off.

The Mets . . . the pesky, tenth-place, futile Mets . . . hurt us and hurt us bad. These are the teams you have to beat if you expect to win a pennant. We played them a doubleheader in New York and counted on winning both games and picking up some ground to put us in a good position for our three-game series with the Phillies. It never fails. When you look ahead of a team and take them too lightly, that's when you get hurt. We beat the Mets in the first game, a 2–1 struggle. But they came back in the second game and beat us, 2–1, in the ninth inning. We were crushed. For the umpty-umpth time we were counted out of the race and the Phillies were home free.

A wise man once said a baseball takes funny bounces. It

certainly bounced right for us. The Phillies had lost 3 straight to Cincinnati, but we couldn't take full advantage of it. We were five games out with eleven games to play and a five-game series against the tough Pittsburgh Pirates staring us in the face.

We still didn't believe we were going to win the pennant. We were looking for second place, really. We knew we had an outside chance, but it was remote. Nobody is going to lose 6 or 7 games in a row when they are that close to the pennant. You have to luck up and win one, and that's the way we figured it, that the Phillies wouldn't fall flat on their face. We had to depend on Philadelphia to keep losing and give us a chance to be close enough when we met them head-to-head. We wanted that series to mean something. That was all we were hoping for.

The way things turned out, we beat the Pirates 5 straight and, at the same time, Milwaukee beat Philadelphia 4 straight. What are the odds on that happening? Maybe 10,000-to-1.

I got us started by beating the Pirates, 4–2, in the first game of a doubleheader and Sadecki shut them out in the second game. Now we were 3½ out with nine games to play and we were still talking second place, although we were all thinking first place. With a week left we still couldn't imagine overtaking them.

Then Gordon Richardson filled in as a starter and gave us a lift by beating Pittsburgh. Curt Simmons won the fourth game and Roger Craig wrapped it up for us and made it 5-for-5 by shutting them out.

And that is just the way it was for us down the stretch, everybody helping out. You couldn't point to one guy and say, "He carried us." Everybody did his share . . . Boyer, White, Groat, Flood, Brock, Shannon, McCarver. During the stretch none of the opposing pitchers lasted more than three or four innings against us. We just mashed them. And our pitching was great.

Roger Craig, who had come over from the Mets, was a

With two weeks to go in 1964, we would have been satisfied with second place, but we didn't stop trying. *Emmons*

great help as a spot starter and reliever. We also got a tremendous amount of help from a most unexpected source. Barney Schultz was a thirty-eight-year-old knuckleball pitcher who had been in baseball for twenty years. He was up and down with several major-league teams and he spent most of the 1964 season with our Jacksonville farm team.

Barney came to us on August 1 and what he did was unbelievable. He was just about our entire bullpen, he and Craig. Old Barney had a natural curiosity and I suppose that helped make him a good pitcher. He never stopped asking questions —about this hitter and that hitter. His curiosity extended outside of baseball too. If you bought a new car, for example, Barney wanted to know everything about it. How it ran, what was in it, how much it cost, everything.

You can't single out one man, of course, but Barney played a big part in our drive. From the time he came up he won only 1 game, but he saved 11. If it hadn't been for him, who knows where we would have been. We'd go into the last inning or two and if we were in trouble Barney would come right in and close the door.

So we beat the Pirates those 5 games and the whole thing heated up. Everything was going just right for us, which is the way it has to happen if you are going to make up that much ground. Now we had the Phillies where we wanted them, coming into St. Louis for a three-game series and leading us by a game and a half. But suddenly, instead of trying to catch one team, we were trying to catch two. Cincinnati had put together a 9-game winning streak and had slipped past Philadelphia into first place. As we started the series with the Phillies, the standings looked like this:

	W.	L.	Games Behind	Games To Play
Cincinnati	91	66	——	5
Philadelphia	90	67	1	5
St. Louis	89	67	1½	6

Suddenly we were in the strange position of not being able to do it ourselves. We had hoped for this head-to-head meeting with Philadelphia to settle things, but now we needed help and we needed it from the Pirates, the team we had just beaten 5 straight. They were playing the Reds three games and we were dependent on Pittsburgh to help us win a pennant, and that is the great thing about the game of baseball. We had humiliated Pittsburgh in five games, yet we knew they would be playing as determinedly against the Reds as if the pennant were theirs to win.

The Pirates were superb. They shut out Cincinnati in two-straight games, the second one in sixteen innings. The Reds failed to score against them for 36 consecutive innings. Cincinnati won the third game of their series, but we couldn't complain. The Pirates did what we hoped they would. Meanwhile, we kept right on rolling.

I pitched the first game against the Phillies and we won, 5–1. Bill White got three singles and knocked in his 94th run of the year, 64 since the All-Star game. Mike Shannon drove in 3 runs. When I tired, Barney Schultz—good old reliable Barney—picked me up in the ninth inning. We don't ordinarily hit Chris Short that well, but he was pitching out of turn, that's how desperate the Phillies were, and his stuff was not as good as it usually is against us.

After that game we thought we could probably win the pennant. We kept right on going in the second game, jumping them early, and we won again. We were up and they were down and we just kept going and they couldn't stop their slide. It happens like that in baseball. Momentum, it's a very important thing.

We made it three straight over the Phillies and they limped out of town. They were finished. Ten straight defeats for them, 8-straight victories for us. Now we were on top and we believed we would win it all. But the situation took another unusual turn. We had three games left with those Mets again and we still needed help. And from whom? From the Phila-

delphia Phillies, who were playing the Cincinnati Reds in the
final two games of the season.

As we prepared to meet the Mets, the standings looked like
this:

	W.	L.	Games Behind	Games To Play
St. Louis	92	67	———	3
Cincinnati	92	68	½	2
Philadelphia	90	70	2½	2

It was my turn to pitch the opening game against the Mets,
played on a Friday night. Al Jackson pitched for the Mets. I
pitched a pretty good game, but Al pitched a better one. We
couldn't handle him at all. He kept throwing that ball down
and away. He always pitched good against us. He was quite
a pitcher for a last-place club.

Jackson beat us, 1–0. I am not an easy loser. When I lose
a tough game I come home and I don't want to talk to anybody. My wife and kids know enough to leave me alone. But
I have never known a loss that was harder to take than that
one against the Mets that Friday night. The one consolation
was when we heard that the Phillies came back to beat the
Reds, 4–3, and our half-game lead was intact. It only made
me feel worse. If I had won, we really would be sitting pretty.

How could you believe a finish like this? Here were the
Phillies, blowing a six-game lead in two weeks, coming back
to knock off the Reds, who only had to keep winning to go
all the way. And here were the Mets, forty games out of first
place, beating a team that had just won 8-straight against
the toughest competition in the league and under the most
crucial circumstances.

It couldn't happen again . . . but it did. On Saturday, the
Reds and Phillies were not scheduled and the Mets beat us
again. They just ran right through us and won, 15–5. We were

never really in the game. We couldn't do anything right. We made errors and they hit the ball all over the place.

Now we were down to the final day. We had played 161 games of a 162-game schedule and we came down to the final day all tied with Cincinnati. A playoff seemed inevitable, and we would have been happy with a tie.

Curt Simmons started for us against Galen Cisco. Before a pitch was thrown, Keane sent me to the bullpen just in case. I had pitched in four of the last nine games and I was tired, mentally and physically, but I knew I would be ready if they needed me. What would they save me for? The playoff? The World Series? We had to win this game first.

The Mets were stubborn. They scored early against Curt, but we tied it up, 1–1. It was obvious Simmons was laboring. In the second inning the Mets threatened again and the telephone rang in the bullpen. Bob Milliken, one of our coaches, answered it, talked for a while, then shouted to me.

"How do you feel, Hoot?"

"I feel all right," I said.

"OK, get up and start throwing."

We went ahead, 2–1, in the fourth, but the Mets scored 2 in the fifth on a windblown double. Two runs were in, they were ahead, 3–2, and the telephone rang in the bullpen again. Milliken picked it up. This time he just listened.

"You're in there, Hoot," he said.

I walked into the game. I wasn't concerned about having only one day of rest. I still felt pretty good. Johnny Keane and Simmons were waiting for me at the mound.

"Go as hard as you can for as long as you can," John said. "We'll have Barney ready in case you need him."

"Good luck, Hoot," Simmons said as he slapped me on the rear and walked off.

I got out of the inning. In the bottom of the fifth we scored 3 runs to go ahead, 5–3, and now we could feel the thing turning for us. At almost the very moment we went ahead, there was another big roar from the crowd. For the past few days we had been kind of looking over our shoulders at the scoreboard, and now on the board was good news—the Phillies had gone ahead of the Reds, 4–0.

That seemed to be the spark we needed. We pounded the Mets for 3 more runs and an 8–4 lead, and the Phillies opened up a 9–0 lead over the Reds, and now the fans in St. Louis were cheering with every pitch and the players were pacing nervously, waiting to unloose the joy that had been building up in them for weeks.

The game in Cincinnati ended. The Phillies beat them, 10–0, and we started the ninth inning leading, 11–4. Nothing could stop us now. I wanted to finish the game, but I was tired. I could hardly stand up.

The Mets would not go down quietly. They put together a couple of hits and scored a run to make it 11–5 and Keane came out to the mound.

"Great job, Hoot," he said. "Better let Barney get the last two outs."

As much as I wanted to finish, I was too tired to argue. And I knew John was doing the right thing.

The ovation as I walked off the field sounded good. I slipped into my warmup jacket and sat on the bench to watch the finish. Barney got the second out, and then Ed Kranepool hit a little pop fly that Tim McCarver caught and the place went wild. Just absolutely, uncontrollably wild. The Cardinals were National League champions for the first time in eighteen years.

To get to our clubhouse in the old St. Louis ball park, we had to walk up a flight of stairs that passed over a long, open corridor under the stands. The stairs were fenced off and on top of them was a landing, like a balcony, that led to the clubhouse. By the time I got up to that landing I could see the corridor was beginning to fill with people, happy, cheering people. Before you knew it the whole corridor was filled with people standing shoulder to shoulder, a mass of humanity covering the entire area. There must have been two or three thousand people there and they just did not want to go home.

They kept cheering and chanting for the players to come out on that landing. "We want Brock! We want Brock!" they shouted, and they wouldn't stop until Lou went out on the landing and waved to them or said something to them.

"We want Boyer! We want Boyer!"

"We want White! . . ."

They kept it up until every player went out on the landing. I was inside near my locker talking to reporters when I heard them chanting, "We want Gibson! We want Gibson! We want Gibson! . . ."

"Hey, Hoot," somebody shouted, "you better go out there before they come up and get you."

I went out on the landing and there was a mighty cheer. I just waved and they cheered again, then I turned back into the clubhouse.

Clubhouse? It was more like a madhouse. Dozens of reporters were jammed into that little room. There were television cameras and radio men, city officials, club officials, celebrities, and some people I didn't even know. The players were having a wild celebration. Champagne corks were popping, and more champagne was going on the floor and on heads and uniforms than was going down the players' throats.

One reporter was talking to Stan Musial.

"Too bad you didn't play one more year, Stan," he said, "so that you could have been a part of this."

"If I had played one more year," Musial answered, "we wouldn't have won the pennant, because then we wouldn't have traded for Lou Brock."

The clubhouse celebration lasted for almost three hours. Like the fans, we didn't want to go home, either. It was a great feeling and we all wanted to savor it.

At the time, nobody was thinking about statistics or trying to grasp exactly what we had accomplished. We were happy, we were enjoying ourselves, we won the pennant. That was all that mattered. The how and the why of it didn't catch up with us for a few months. As I look back, it was really amazing.

We won 28 of our last 39 games. Bill White knocked in 72 runs in the second half to finish with 102. Lou Brock batted .348 after he joined us. Ray Sadecki won 20 games, twice as many as the previous year, and Curt Simmons won 18. Personally, I was very pleased with my season. I won 14 games after the All-Star break, 4 more than Bing Devine asked for. I won 9 of my last 11 decisions and had 8-straight complete games in that stretch.

My victory in relief on the final day was my nineteenth. I should have had my first 20-game season. Back in May I got tossed out of a game against Philadelphia for throwing my bat after I was hit by a pitch. We were ahead, 7-1, in the fourth inning. We won the game, but I didn't get credit for the victory, which would have given me 20.

Sure, I would have liked to have won 20, but winning 20 cannot compare with winning the pennant. That was the most thrilling thing that ever happened to me. I never experienced anything like it before or since and I don't ever expect to experience anything like it again.

Dick Groat and I celebrate our pennant clinching with a bottle of the bubbly, most of it over us.   *UPI*

CHAPTER 9   *YANKEES, NO!*

A week before we would have been happy with second-place money and suddenly we were in the World Series. We hardly had time to prepare and we were too numb to even think about playing in the Series.

It is hard to think of the World Series as an anticlimax, but after the exciting conclusion to the pennant race, that's what it was . . . for a while. We were just happy to be in it.

It hits you all at once. It begins building up within you the day before the first game. It starts with an avalanche of requests for tickets and that gets you to realizing this is something special. Then it is the day of the opening game and the thrill of it is like nothing else you ever experience in baseball.

I don't know what it is. The big crowds. The hundreds of reporters, photographers, and television men. The flags decorating the stadium. The thought of all that money involved. The presence of celebrities. Whatever it is, you suddenly feel the excitement of it all and nothing that happened before is important. The only thing you think of is the team you're playing, and the only thing that matters is beating them in this game, today.

Our opponents were the New York Yankees. In those days if you won the National League pennant you always met the

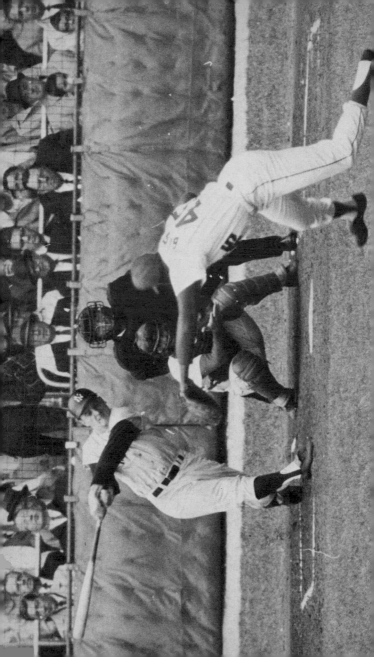

Yankees in the World Series. We were high and we figured we could beat anybody. After going over our scouting reports, we were sure we would beat the Yankees.

We knew Mickey Mantle had a bad knee and couldn't get around too well. They had Roger Maris playing center field, which was not his normal position, and the reports on Tom Tresh were that he was not an exceptional fielder, so we figured we could do a lot of running and take the extra base against them.

What I noticed more than anything else was that our scouting reports on Mantle said pitch him inside whether he was batting right-handed or left-handed because he likes to get his arms out over the plate. But I pitched him outside the whole Series and he didn't hurt me until the last game when he hit a home run to left field. By then we were way ahead. I'm sure he was having trouble with his knee because I noticed when I pitched him outside and he had to reach out his knee would buckle a little, so he didn't want to reach out and go after it. He wouldn't swing as hard at the ball away from him as he did at the ball inside, so I kept it away and had good success. That tells you something about scouting reports.

I must admit the Yankees did not impress me very much. In the first game we came from behind with 4 runs in the fifth. We beat them 9–5, with Barney Schultz saving the victory for Ray Sadecki.

It was my turn to work the second game against Mel Stottlemyre, a rookie and a good-looking one. Stottlemyre was sharp, keeping the ball low, but I was throwing good too. I struck out five batters in the first two innings.

The turning point in the game, I believe, came in the sixth inning. The score was 1–1 when Joe Pepitone came to bat. Mantle, who walked, was on first. The count went to 1–2 on Pepitone and I tried to jam him with a fast ball. The pitch came close to him and umpire Bill McKinley said it hit him on the right thigh. Funny, because Pepitone later said it hit him

The Yankee batter in the '64 Series is Roger Maris—three seasons before he became my Cardinal teammate. *UPI*

on the left thigh. As he went down to first base he was rubbing both thighs—and laughing. When I saw him the following spring I asked him if the ball hit him and he laughed again. He never answered me. To this day, I still think the ball never hit him.

But he was on first and Mantle was on second and the next batter, Tresh, hit a ball past the shortstop for a run and a 2–1 lead. I went out of the game for a pinch-hitter and the Yankees scored 6 runs after I was out, to win 8–3.

The third game was a tough one for us and especially for Barney Schultz. Curt Simmons and Jim Bouton battled for eight innings tied, 1–1, then Curt was removed for a pinch-hitter in the ninth. Barney came in to pitch the last of the ninth and Mantle hit his first pitch for a game-winning home run. We felt bad for Barney, who had done so much to help us win the pennant.

We got even in the fourth game. Again we had to come from behind. The Yankees jumped out to a 3–0 lead against Sadecki, but Roger Craig held them while we went ahead on Kenny Boyer's grand-slam homer in the sixth. Ron Taylor finished up to save the victory for Rog, 4–3.

Dick Groat said the background in Yankee Stadium was the worst he ever hit against. In the fall, especially late in the day, shadows begin gathering around home plate and by the middle of the game most of the infield is in shadows. The batter has a hard time seeing, looking out from the dark into all those light shirts in the center-field bleachers. I loved it. That is probably the reason I got so many strikeouts in the fifth game—12 of them.

Here is where an overreliance on scouting reports worked in my favor. They said I threw mostly fast balls, so while the Yankees were looking for the high fast ball, I was throwing probably 80 percent breaking balls, which were down. I wasn't strong because I had pitched four games in the last eight days, but my ball was moving good and I was keeping it down.

My basketball jumping ability came in handy when the Yankees' Hector Lopez accidentally let go of his bat.

I had them beat, 2–0, going into the ninth inning. Mantle led off and he topped a ball to shortstop. Groat charged it, then bobbled it, and Mantle was safe. After Elston Howard struck out, Pepitone lined one back off my hip. Luckily, I didn't stop to think about the pain. I scrambled for the ball and my throw to first just beat him.

With two out Tresh hit one into the right-field bleachers to tie it, and there are those scouting reports again. Our reports said pitch Tresh inside. I did. He hit it into the seats.

Fortunately, Tim McCarver picked me—and Groat—up with a three-run homer in the tenth and we won, 5–2. I hoped I had pitched my last game of the year, but the Yankees wouldn't let me rest. They evened the Series with an 8–3 victory in the sixth game and I had to work again. Keane named me to pitch the seventh game in St. Louis against Mel Stottlemyre with only two days' rest. At least one thing was certain. After this game I would have a whole winter to rest.

For three-and-a-half innings we played scoreless ball. Then we scored 3 runs in the fourth and 3 more in the fifth when Lou Brock homered and White and Boyer doubled. We led 6–0. I had to hold on for four more innings and we would be world champions.

I was tired, but with a big lead I figured I could get by with nothing but fast balls. Mantle hit a 3-run home run in the sixth and things got a little sticky. I half-expected Keane to come walking out of the dugout and I was happy when he didn't.

I got by the seventh and Boyer gave me a breather with a home run in the eighth to give us a 7–3 lead.

Just one more inning. Three more outs. Fast balls would do it, I thought. Let them hit it. They can't hit four home runs off me in one inning. Oh, can't they?

Tresh struck out and Clete Boyer hit a home run. John Blanchard struck out and Phil Linz hit a home run. Now it was 7–5. But that was a fair exchange, an out for a home run. At that rate I'd still win. But Keane wasn't taking any chances.

I'm not very happy after giving up a homer to that man (Mickey Mantle) circling the bases.

He had Barney Schultz ready in the bullpen, and John was on his way out to the mound.

"How do you feel, Hoot?" he asked.

"I feel fine," I lied.

I wouldn't have cared if I was keeling over out there, I never would say I was tired. You never feel you're not the right guy to do the job unless you're hurt. It goes with having confidence in yourself. You could be out on your feet and they could be beating your brains out and you still think you're the best and you can get them out. This is the feeling you have to have. Very few guys give up, and that's what you would be doing if you told the manager you were tired; you would be giving up. It's very seldom that a manager takes your word anyway. He knows what he wants to do when he comes out there and Keane wanted me to stay.

"I want you to finish this," he said.

Fine. That's what I wanted too. I later found out the man at bat was going to be my last man, whether I got him out or not. The two batters after him were Maris and Mantle and Keane didn't want a tired pitcher facing those sluggers, especially in our ball park with that inviting right-field screen.

The hitter was Bobby Richardson, who was hitting pretty good all Series, especially against me. I was pitching him wrong. The scouting reports had instructed us to pitch him away and he kept wearing me out by hitting the ball back through the middle. McCarver had a suggestion.

"He's been hitting the ball away pretty good," Tim said. "Let's try something different. Let's come in on him."

By this time I had lost all faith in scouting reports and I was willing to try something different, so I quickly agreed.

"Yeah," I said, "that's a pretty good idea. We'll come in on him."

I threw him a fast ball in tight and he hit it off his fists and popped it up on the right side of the infield.

"Don't let it hit you on the coconut, Max," Groat shouted.

It's all over. We've won it and Ken Boyer and I whoop it up.
UPI

And Dal Maxvill didn't. He squeezed that ball and everybody went wild. We were world champions.

It was another wild clubhouse celebration with the champagne and television cameras and well-wishers and everything, although not as wild as when we clinched the pennant. I guess we were all too tired.

My wife was waiting outside on the stairs and I went out and hugged her. She was crying.

One reporter told me I had set a World Series record for strikeouts with 31. Another told me something Johnny Keane said about me, something that made me feel proud. This reporter had asked John why he didn't take me out of the game when it was obvious I was tiring and they were catching up.

"I was committed to his heart," John said.

It is probably the nicest thing that can be said about an athlete and I will always remember it. I will also remember what John said to me after the game. We had come into the clubhouse before any of the reporters or television people entered and John came to me and threw his arms around me and hugged me.

"You're on your way, Hoot," he said. "Nothing can stop you now."

I'm clowning around in the Cardinal clubhouse . . . always a lively place. *UPI*

CHAPTER 10 *THE HERO*

The plane roared into Omaha, taxied up to the terminal, and pulled to a stop. As we were getting off, I spotted them. There must have been a dozen or more of them. Photographers. Reporters.

I spotted the cameras first. Rather they spotted me. As soon as I stuck my head out of the plane the flashbulbs began to explode. The price of fame, I thought smugly. I shouldn't have been so smug. I should have realized that all those photographers and reporters would not have turned out at the airport just to record the home-town hero's triumphant return.

"What do you think about Johnny Keane?" one of the reporters shouted as soon as I was within earshot.

"I think he's a decent man and a fine manager," I said, a little surprised by the question.

"Yes, but what do you think about him resigning?"

That one pulled me up short. For the moment, I didn't speak. I kept remembering what John had said to me in the clubhouse after the seventh game. "You're on your way, Hoot. Nothing can stop you now."

I should have realized something was up. If I had thought

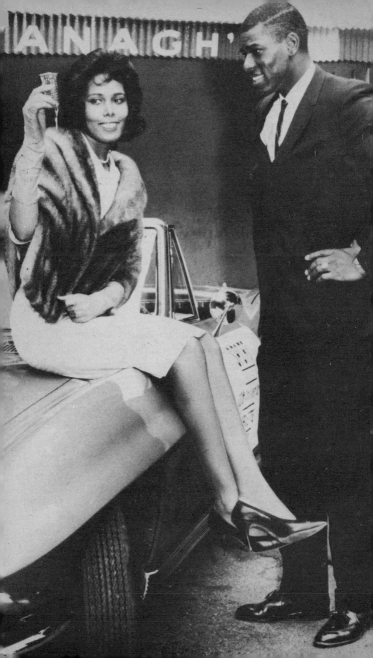

about it I might have realized it, but I was too preoccupied with my own hectic schedule. We had flown to Omaha from St. Louis for a "Bob Gibson Day" celebration and we were scheduled to go back to New York the next day so that I could pick up my Corvette, presented each year by *Sport* magazine to the player selected the outstanding performer in the World Series.

We had all known there was something cooking with Keane as far back as August. On August 18, Bing Devine was dropped as general manager and replaced by Bob Howsam. We had not yet started to make our big move and it was ironic that the big difference in our club toward the end of the season was Lou Brock, the man Devine had traded for. It was also ironic that Bing was not around at the end to enjoy watching "his team" win the pennant. By then he was working for the New York Mets.

At the time Devine was let go, rumors were flying all around about Keane. Some reports even said Leo Durocher had already been contacted and offered the job as Cardinal manager. Naturally, when we came on at the end, we all assumed John had saved his job—and he probably did. We never imagined he would walk out on it.

Sure I was shocked. Perhaps "surprised" is a better word, because in baseball you learn never to be shocked by anything. The more I thought about it, though, the less surprised I was, and I told reporters so.

"Johnny Keane is a person with a lot of character," I said. "He never took anything from anybody. If he thought he was right and you were wrong about a certain thing, he was not going to tell you different, no matter who you happened to be. I wish him luck in whatever he does."

It was the next day that the announcement came that Keane had been hired to manage the Yankees. As I told the reporters, Keane is a proud man, a man of principle. I guess all the rumors about him being fired and the club's reluctance

This is the Corvette I won from Sport Magazine . . . and Charline's got the keys.

to sign him for 1965 got him down and he walked out on them.

One of the reporters asked me if I thought, since Johnny and I were so close, that his absence would affect my pitching.

Now, that's silly. I'm a professional ballplayer. I've got to go out there and do my job no matter who the manager is. Sure, there are some managers you like playing for better than others, but it never affects your performance. You're still going to be judged by how much you produce. If I have a lousy year I'm not going to get a raise just because the manager likes me. If I have a good year I'm not going to get cut because the manager dislikes me.

You come to expect these things in baseball. Your best friend might get traded. What can you do? I might get traded some day. But I'm doing this for a living. I'm not going to sit back and worry about it or brood about it if it happens. I'd like to play with the Cardinals for the rest of my career, but if I got traded I would be disappointed for about ten minutes, then I would look forward to playing with my new team and having a good year. People get fired, get traded, or quit all the time.

I was going to miss John, but you get used to these things. I think you can get used to almost anything. I think you could probably get used to dying if you did it more than once.

I am not an emotional person. When I have a feeling of happiness or sadness or disappointment or anything, it doesn't linger long with me. I don't dwell on it. It passes quickly, and the idea that I would not be playing for Johnny Keane anymore passed quickly. Besides, I was too busy that winter to think about it, although not as busy as I thought I would be.

I don't know what I expected. A lot of people told me that as the so-called "hero" of the World Series I could expect to do all right. Things usually opened up for the player who was so designated. The year before, Sandy Koufax won 2 games in the World Series and set a strikeout record and he had any number of appearances and endorsements. I was counting on making a lot of extra money.

I made hardly any money at all. I got my expenses paid to a couple of banquets, I made an appearance on one television show, I got the Corvette from *Sport* magazine and I got a trip to the Rose Bowl game. Tim McCarver had been married on Christmas day and he and his bride, and Charline and I, were invited to spend a week in California, to see the Rose Bowl game, and to ride on the Budweiser float in the Rose Bowl parade. We spent two-and-a-half hours on the thing. It was a nice vacation for us and I don't mean to sound ungrateful, but I considered it a small reward for being the "star" of the World Series.

That was all there was. Not at all what I had been led to believe. I think there were two reasons why I did not reap the benefits of the World Series. For one, I had no agent, nobody pushing for me. For another, as a Negro I was not considered a desirable commodity for commercial endorsements.

Things had changed in the Cardinal camp in the spring of 1965. Our new manager was Red Schoendienst and Bob Howsam had assumed full command as general manager.

Red was a lot like Keane. He had been a coach under John and I knew him as a decent man, soft-spoken and easy-going, many thought too soft-spoken and easy-going. Howsam? He was something else again.

I felt bad when Bing Devine left. I thought he was probably the best general manager in either league as far as his treatment of players was concerned. I couldn't imagine one being any better. Bing was really for the ballplayer. Most general managers are organization men, but Devine was pretty close to us.

Howsam, on the other hand, was a difficult man to understand. He tried to run a baseball club the way you would run an elementary-school classroom. He would send memoran-

The Omaha Chamber of Commerce had a Bob Gibson Day. ⟶

31
STRIKE-OUTS
ALL-TIME
WORLD SERIES
RECORD

dums down to the clubhouse that a player was slouching too much on the bench or wearing his pants too low. Once he had a newspaper article pinned on the bulletin board about Willie Stargell being able to hit the ball to the opposite field with power. I guess he was trying to give some of our hitters ideas about not trying to pull every ball. What he should have done was go out and get Willie Stargell. Needless to say the article didn't stay on the bulletin board too long. Howsam was nice as an individual, but some of his ideas on running a baseball team were strange.

I can't think of anything good to say about the 1965 season, even though I won 20 games for the first time in my career and struck out 270 batters, third highest in the league. As I said before, winning 20 games means nothing if you are playing on a losing team. We finished seventh, 16½ games out of first place.

How can a team win the pennant one year and finish seventh the next with the same personnel? If you can find the answer to that one you can become rich overnight. Nobody knows how a thing like that happens. Just as everything went right for us in the second half of 1964, everything went wrong for us all through 1965. And, just as it is impossible to single out one player as totally responsible for a good season, it is impossible to single one out as totally responsible for a bad year.

Curt Simmons and Ray Sadecki had won 38 games between them in 1964. In 1965, they won 15. Bill White and Ken Boyer had knocked in 221 runs between them in 1963. In 1964, they knocked in 148. Mike Shannon's average dropped 40 points; Dick Groat lost 38 points; Boyer 35; Lou Brock 27; White 14. It was just one of those years.

There were more changes on the Cardinals in 1966 . . . a lot more. Howsam really cleaned house. He traded Ken Boyer to the New York Mets for Charlie Smith and Al Jackson. And he traded Bill White, Dick Groat, and Bob Uecker

Red Schoendienst, my third manager in the big leagues, is a lot like Johnny Keane. *UPI*

to the Philadelphia Phillies for Alex Johnson, Pat Corrales, and Art Mahaffey.

I thought the Boyer trade was all right because I always liked Al Jackson as a pitcher and I figured Smith could produce what Boyer had produced at bat in 1965. Personally, I was sorry to see Kenny go. We had always been fairly close. I used to kid him all the time.

For some reason the St. Louis fans would get on him whenever he went to bat. I could never understand it because he was such an outstanding player for so many years, but I knew that as soon as they announced his name everybody would boo. So when they started to announce his name I'd yell, loud enough for him to hear, "One . . . two . . . three . . ." Then the boos would come, and Kenny would just turn around and laugh at me.

The other trade made no sense to me at all. For White, Groat, and Uecker you could get a lot. I'm sure somebody would have wanted a Bill White enough to have given up half a team for him alone. You just don't come up with some young ballplayer nobody knows, such as Alex Johnson. And that was all it amounted to. They wanted Johnson. He was a good prospect, but a prospect, that's all. He had never accomplished anything in the big leagues and to give up a Bill White and Dick Groat for him . . . well, I just don't think we got enough in return.

They tried to say it was a youth movement, but I don't think that was the real reason. I think the reason for the trades was that Bob Howsam was trying to cut the payroll. He got rid of Boyer, White, and Groat, the three highest-paid players on the team. I figured I was the next one to go.

Statistically I had a pretty good year. I won 21 and lost 12 and had a 2.44 earned-run average. But it was a miserable year for two reasons. Just before the All-Star game I tore something in my elbow and was out of action for fifteen days. I had been pitching with three days' rest and my arm got tired, but I kept pitching. Joe Becker, our pitching coach, kept telling me my arm was not strong enough, that I had to throw between starts to strengthen it. I don't like to throw between starts and I like four days' rest, so my arm just got too tired and I tore something and dropped out of the rotation.

Rest, diathermy, massage, and soaking it in ice got the arm strong again. At the time I hurt myself, my record was 11–10. In the second half I won 10 and lost 2.

Again we finished down the ladder, in sixth place twelve games out of first. The season was no fun. I have played with winners and I have played with losers and, believe me, winning is better.

Two good things happened that season, both in the month of May. On May 12, we moved into the new Busch Stadium, which turned out to be a pitcher's paradise. It's 330 feet down the lines and 414 feet in center field. You've got to really poke the ball to get it out of there. If you hit a home run in that park you deserve it. That was the reason I allowed only 20 home runs in 1966, 14 fewer than the year before.

The other good thing came as an indirect result of the Bill White trade. I guess Howsam realized he left us powerless, so when the opportunity to obtain Orlando Cepeda presented itself, Howsam took advantage of it. We gave up Ray Sadecki. If we still had White, I'm sure we would not have made the trade.

We were able to get Orlando because he had had an operation on his knee during the winter and because Willie McCovey had taken over the Giants' first-base job, and because Cepeda and Giant manager Herman Franks could not see eye-to-eye.

Orlando came to us on May 6 and gave us the big bat we needed so desperately. He batted .301, hit 20 home runs and drove in 73 runs for the season. We were to hear a lot more from him later.

CHAPTER 11 *THE HOUSE I LIVE IN*

I went to school and I read my history books and I always believed in that stuff—life, liberty, and the pursuit of happiness. I believed in the land of the free and the home of the brave. I believed in the free-enterprise system. I believed that if you wanted something badly enough all you had to do was work for it, and if you could afford it, you could buy it. I naïvely believed all these things. Then I tried to buy a house in an all-white neighborhood.

I had put together four pretty good years, winning 78 games in that span, and now I was beginning to get up in the higher-income bracket. I had the money to spend and I was willing to spend it.

Late in the 1966 season, my wife called me and said she had found a house she liked, and I told her if she liked it to go ahead and put a down payment on it. We had planned to build our house, but the bids were ridiculously high—between $88,000 and $100,000 for a house that, according to my architect, should have cost no more than $45,000 or $50,000.

I was the victim of prejudice. I'm not saying it was because I am a Negro. I'm not sure that was the reason and I don't like to say anything I'm not sure of. But if it wasn't that, it was because I am a baseball player. Everybody thinks a baseball player is rich and they try to raise the price on you. That's prejudice against baseball players, and I hate prejudice in any form.

So Charline liked this house in the Rockbrook Park section of Omaha, an all-white neighborhood, and I told her to buy it. I don't want to live next door to you just because you're white. I was living in the ghetto and I wanted to move into a nice house in a nice neighborhood, and you know where you can get nice houses? Out of the ghetto. In an all-white neighborhood.

Why do you move out of the ghetto? Because it's the ghetto. I want the better things in life just like everybody else. I want a nice house. I want to enjoy the things I worked hard to be able to afford. Am I not supposed to want these things for myself? For my wife? For my children? Am I any different than any other husband and father just because my face is black?

There are white people living in the ghetto who want to move out, but it's a big deal when I do it. It's not a big deal when a white man wants to do it. But when I want to move in there, it's a Negro moving into a white neighborhood and wanting to disrupt things. If there are ten houses on a street and one or two Negro families move in, why do the white families have to move out? I'd like to see a law against it, but there is no way to do that, so . . .

If I pay $50,000 or $60,000 for a house, I'm going to take care of it just like the guy next door takes care of his. If I couldn't afford it, I wouldn't be living there in the first place. This idea that a Negro will neglect his property and run down the neighborhood all stems from the false notion that a Negro is, in some way, inferior. It is a stereotype that goes back to the time of slavery, just like the idea that all Negroes carry knives and all Negroes are shiftless and lazy and not very bright. We've got to break down these stereotypes. If somebody lives next door to you and you get to know him, you won't have to guess what he's like. Chances are you'll find out you had the wrong idea about him.

Negroes aren't the only ones who downgrade an area. Maybe some poor ones do, but there are an awful lot of white people who are undesirable and who neglect their property and run down a neighborhood. But they would never be denied the right to move into any neighborhood. I would.

I think a check of the Federal Housing Administration would show that there are a greater percentage of whites who never finish paying for their homes than there are Negroes, and that very few Negroes have their homes repossessed.

Another stereotype is that the Negro likes to drive a big car even though he cannot afford a nice place to live in. Let's consider that for a moment. The Negro likes to have value for his money. He wants to have something a little better. He wants to go first class because this is an improvement, a better way to live than what he is accustomed to. This is not a stereotype. Everybody wants to go first class if he can. The Negro cannot afford to join a country club and he can't go to Miami, and most of them cannot buy a $60,000 house. But he can buy an $8,000 car. This is one of the better things in life. If he can't buy a $60,000 house—if the best he can afford is a $15,000 house—then he will buy the next best thing, a big, expensive car. That will be one of the big things in his life.

I remember taking my girls for dinner in a restaurant about five years ago. My oldest girl, Renee, said, "Daddy, how come whenever we go to a restaurant we never see any other colored people?"

I tried to explain to her that Daddy is a little more fortunate than the average Negro.

Charline and I talked it over before we decided to buy this house. She was concerned about the children, about the problems they would have, the things they would have to put up with. I told her somebody was going to have to suffer if we moved there and it might be the children. I said if she wanted them to be completely accepted, then we would just stay where we were, in the ghetto. At the time they were no better off than I was as a kid. When I lived in the slum, I didn't know it was a slum. I didn't know any better. But when they got older, then they'd realize it and they might resent it that we kept them in the ghetto. We talked this over, and we talked to the girls too. We told them what they might expect, what they would have to put up with, and we all agreed to make the move.

Most of the people in the neighborhood were indifferent when they heard we were moving in, but there were some who wanted to keep us out. The people who built the house had hired somebody to come and finish painting it, and one neighbor talked him into quitting in the middle of the job, so we had to get another painter to finish up.

Later on this same neighbor apologized and turned out to be a pretty fair neighbor.

We have one neighbor across the street who is from Massachusetts and who is exceptionally decent. He and his family are beautiful people. He moved in after we did and we have become good friends. He said that when he bought his house somebody told him, "There's a Negro living across the street, but it's *only* Bob Gibson, the ballplayer."

There are a lot of places that accept me because I'm Bob Gibson the ballplayer but wouldn't accept me if I were Bob Gibson, machine-shop worker or clerk or trucker. It doesn't excite me when I go into a restaurant and they give me the glad hand because I'm Bob Gibson the ballplayer. I know that's the reason they do that. They might throw the next Negro out. They're not accepting me because I'm an individual, only because I'm a known individual. Even now I can go into a place and get a cold reception, then they find out who you are and they change like night and day. I've experienced that.

I take people as I see them. I can talk with them a little while and know if they are sincere and if they like Negroes or not. I walked into a place once dressed up with a suit and tie and a lady asked me if I was a minister.

"Why?" I said. "Because I'm not dirty?"

I think I insulted her. Too bad. She insulted me with her question. Other than being a baseball player, all I am is another person, just like you. At least I should be. Everybody is on the same level, they just refuse to admit it.

When we first moved into this new neighborhood, my girls had problems. I knew they would. If you're a Negro moving into an all-white area, your kids are going to have problems. My girls got a lot of static at school. Kids are mean. They have a way of saying the wrong thing and usually it is the result of their environment. A child will only reflect his parents' teaching and he will repeat what he hears around his house. On the other hand, children have a way of overcoming these barriers and shrugging off these insults. Usually it's the parents who cause the biggest problems.

We tried to explain to our girls that children sometimes say things they don't mean and don't understand. We told them to try to ignore these slurs and insults, but I never bought that stuff when I was a kid and I knew they wouldn't either.

Renee had a problem with a male teacher. I had to go to school because she came home crying that the teacher had squeezed her behind the neck. Some boy was pulling her foot and calling her names and Renee started to fight with him. A child, even a girl, is going to fight back because all this name-calling irritates. The teacher saw them fighting and before he found out what the fight was all about he punished them. The teacher told Renee if she wanted to fight, he would get her some boxing gloves so she could go and fight with the little boy.

Now you're never sure of anything, but my girls had so much trouble in school that we just had to conclude the problems were racial. They never had any trouble in our immediate area. Most of the problems have been in school, and even these have been less and less lately. Maybe the people have grown used to them and accepted them probably because of who I am. If I were not a baseball player and moved out there, acceptance would be a much slower process, but I think it would come in time. The people get to know you a little better and find out that the opinions they had about Negroes are false. And these are the barriers we must try to break down.

Unfortunately, things move very slowly in most places, particularly in Omaha. It's a great place to live in, to raise children. Not too metropolitan, lots of open spaces and fresh air, but the people are afraid to change. They're used to doing things a certain way and if somebody brings up a bill to change it, they are going to vote it down. It disturbs me. It disturbs Charline more. She is very active in civic affairs. She is a member of the Omaha Human Relations Board, which is trying to right some of the wrongs against Negroes, injustices such as unemployment and terrible housing and schools.

I don't mean to suggest that Omaha is the only place where we encountered problems. We also had them in St. Louis. The first year I was up, I was trying to find a place to live. Harry Caray, who announces the Cardinal games, mentioned it on the radio. He got a call from some woman who said she had a three-bedroom house she wanted to rent to Bob Gibson. Harry told me and I called the woman.

It couldn't have been more than an hour after Harry got the information, but she said she had already rented it. I have to believe that sometime between her call to Harry and my call to her, she found out I was a Negro.

I'm kind of sensitive about things and I might sound as if I have a chip on my shoulder. I do. But I didn't put it there. Somebody else did.

CHAPTER 12 *FOUR MEN*

The year 1967 started out with a thud. On January 6 a reporter called me with some horrible news. Johnny Keane had died.

It is hard to explain your feelings at a time like that. A lot of things go through your mind, memories of things past, silly things. A particular game, a certain situation, a word or a phrase that John said that suddenly comes back to you.

I didn't see much of Johnny after he left the Cardinals, because as manager of the Yankees he was in the other league. We didn't talk much after the day he told me, "You're on your way, Hoot. Nothing can stop you now."

I saw him in spring training and we just said hello. He said, "Hi, Hoot. How's it going?" That was all. I met him a few times at banquets, but there was never time to say anything more than "Hello, how are you? How is the family?"

I followed John's progress with the Yankees and was sorry to see he had so many problems, but you really don't think about that too much. We were having problems of our own. Naturally, I wanted John to do well. Naturally, I wanted us to do well even more, so it was hard to sympathize with another team.

Then Johnny was fired by the Yankees and I felt bad, but I believed he would be back in baseball some day. He was too good a man not to be hired by somebody.

As I said before, I am not an emotional person. When something sad happens, I don't sit and ponder it, I try to block it out of my mind. That's what I did when John died, but I was really sad when I first heard about it. He was the first manager I ever had in professional baseball and he helped me more than anybody else in the game with his encouragement and by giving me a chance to pitch when he took over as manager of the Cardinals.

In a way, the feeling I had when I heard that Johnny Keane died was similar to what I felt on November 22, 1963. I was in my basement putting up some chimes for the doorbell and I had the television set on. Suddenly they interrupted the program to announce that President Kennedy had been shot in Dallas. That was all they said, that he was shot, not that he was killed.

I got down off the ladder and I listened. I was shocked. I could hardly believe it was true. I didn't want to believe it. I kept thinking that at least he was alive and maybe he would pull through. Then the announcement came that he was dead and I felt empty inside. I was sad. My wife started crying. I don't think I ever felt any worse about someone I didn't know, and I think it's strange to have a deep feeling for someone you don't know. Then again, I had the strangest feeling that I did know him, although I had never met President Kennedy. I saw him at the All-Star game in Washington in 1962, but I didn't meet him. He was sitting behind the American League dugout and I was in the National League dugout, and that was as close as I ever got to him, a couple of hundred feet. Still I felt as if I knew him.

Most Negroes felt they knew him because of the job he was trying to do. To finally get somebody who had you in mind, who respected you as a human being, who was trying to do something for you and then, all of a sudden, poof, he is gone . . . well, it made you sad. I think most Negroes had a deep feeling for him.

In many ways, the feeling was similar on the day Dr. Martin
Luther King, Jr. was assassinated. I was in spring training, in
my room, and the television was on but I was not paying close
attention to it. I thought I heard something about Dr. King
being shot, but I wasn't sure. So I went to Lou Brock's room
to check if it was true. Orlando Cepeda was there and from
the expression on their faces, I knew I had heard correctly.

"It's true," Lou said.

It made me very sad. I think the emotions I felt most
strongly were bitterness and frustration . . . just like when
President Kennedy was shot. It seemed that whenever there
is someone going out of his way to do something, to fight for
this cause, something happens to him.

I never had the pleasure of meeting Dr. King, but I did
see him once. I attended a banquet in Atlanta on February
6, 1968, and I walked right by him in the Atlanta airport. I
looked at him and he kind of looked at me as if he recognized
me, but I'm not sure he did. I don't know why he would have.
I wanted to go over and say something to him, but people
are always coming up to me in airports and restaurants and
on the streets. I know how it feels to be disturbed. I was sure
he got that all the time, so I figured I'd just leave him alone.
I'm sorry now that I didn't go over and shake his hand.

I had tremendous admiration for Dr. King, for the great
work he was doing. His was one approach to the problem and
there are others with different approaches and I think you
have to have all types if the fight is to be successful. You have
to have the non-violent and you have to have the violent. If
it could be accomplished the way Martin Luther King wanted
it done, that would be the best way.

I called Charline the night Dr. King died. I knew she would
be feeling pretty bad and she was.

We were scheduled to open the season in St. Louis on the
day Dr. King was buried. The Cardinals asked us if we would
be willing to play and we said no, so they called the game off,

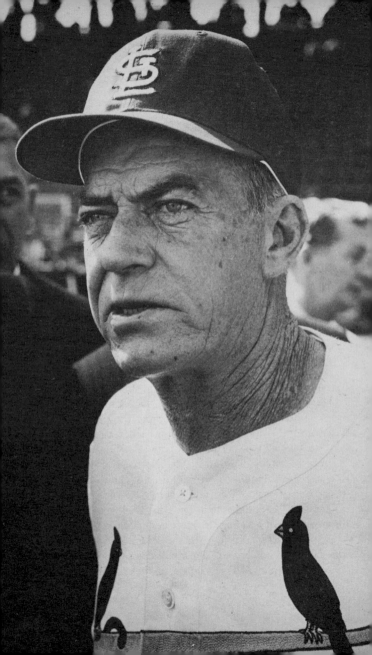

which was the only thing they could do. Some of the white players on the Cardinals felt his death was a shame, but their feeling was not the same as ours. I guess there were more who didn't care one way or the other than there were those who did care and that's the whole trouble—there are too many white people who don't care.

Naturally, Johnny Keane's death was going to affect me more personally than President Kennedy's or even Dr. King's because I knew John. I knew Johnny real well. I had a lot of respect for him not only as a manager, but as a human being as well. I owed him a great deal. I thought Johnny was one of the nicest people I ever met in my life and I really felt sorry when he died. I felt sorry for his wife, whom I knew very well, and for his daughter.

I think Johnny Keane's death probably affected me as much as anybody's I've ever known. I never really knew death before. My father was dead when I was born. I lost an uncle who was very close to me, but I was just a kid at the time, and when you're young you just know that people are gone but you don't really understand why. That was my uncle Nap. He was always very good to us. It seemed like he always had money in his pocket. He worked in the packing house and was not married, so he always had money to give us or to buy us presents with.

I remember that when I was nine or ten I used to go to down-town Omaha to shine shoes so that I could make some extra money. I'd get my little kit and walk around trying to get a customer, but I very rarely got one. I'd never make any money. There were so many kids down there with shoeshine boxes, and it seemed I always got there a day late. So I would go home and I would shine Uncle Nap's shoes and he would give me a half dollar or a dollar, and that made me happy. Then all of a sudden Uncle Nap was gone. As I was growing up I rarely thought about him. Then one day I got a call from a reporter who told me Johnny Keane was dead and I thought about Uncle Nap.

I respected Johnny Keane not only as a manager but as a human being.   *Ken Regan*

CHAPTER 13 *PRESS ON REGARDLESS*

The winter of 1967 we made a few trades, but none got as much attention and publicity as the one which brought Roger Maris to the Cardinals.

Whenever a new player joins a club, particularly a player you don't know, you are always curious to find out just what kind of guy he is. Will he be friendly? Will he be a good teammate? Will he blend in well with the other personalities on the team?

This was especially true of Roger Maris. We had all read and heard so much about him and now we would see for ourselves what he was like. Was he really the brooding, sullen, unapproachable ogre he was made out to be?

In 1961 Maris had the audacity to break Babe Ruth's home-run record when he hit 61. Then the fun began. The press was unmerciful. It was as if he had committed some crime by breaking the record of some sacred cow. How dare he?

Ever since then Maris carried on a running feud with the New York press, which, I suspect, is part of the reason he wound up in St. Louis. Now we would see for ourselves just what kind of monster he was.

I guess I had a preconceived idea of what he would be like from all the derogatory things I'd read about him. I expected

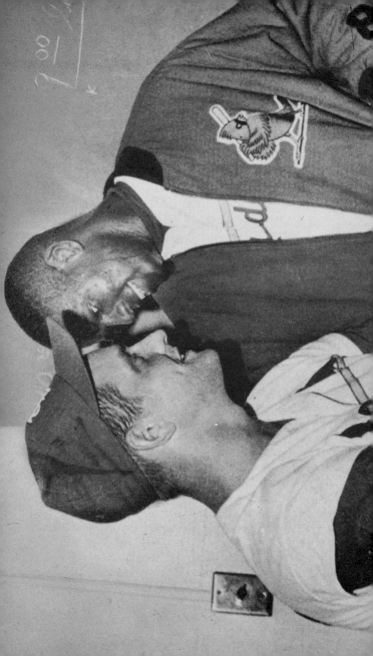

him to be snobbish. I couldn't have been more wrong. From my personal firsthand experience I can only say that Roger Maris is one hell of a guy, easy to get along with and a real team player. I think he's great. He was mistreated and abused so badly he became bitter, but he was not at all like that with us. I don't think he ever got a fair shake from the press when he was in New York. Talking about Roger Maris gives me the opportunity to discuss the boys of the fourth estate, with whom I have had more than my share of innings.

Let me preface my remarks by saying I realize sportswriters have a job to do and they are entitled to do that job to the best of their ability. I have no quarrel with that, I just don't want them to make themselves big, important men at my expense.

I try not to be bothered much by what I read in the newspapers, but there are things reporters do that cannot be ignored, things that really annoy me. They constantly misquote you; they write stories without first checking all the facts; they try to intimidate you into saying something controversial; they ask silly questions.

I don't mean to make a blanket indictment of all reporters. Some are very fair and conscientious in their jobs, and not all of them are guilty of the things I have mentioned. It's unfortunate that when I say "reporters" I am lumping all reporters, the good ones with the bad. But the majority of them are guilty of one of these things or another.

Nothing is worse than to say one thing and have it come out entirely different in the paper. Then if you confront the writer with it, he says, "Well, that's the way I interpreted it." No it isn't. Their business is to sell papers, and that's the way they can sell papers, by misquoting you and getting you to say something controversial.

I read a magazine article once in which the writer quoted me as saying, "I don't do much thinking about pitching, I just rear back and hum dat pea." My wife read it and knew damn well I never said that. She wrote a letter to the magazine be-

After Roger Maris became my teammate, I discovered he was not the ogre the press made him out to be. *UPI*

fore she even talked to me about it because she knew I would never say anything like that and I never use expressions like "hum dat pea."

I have read articles in which I was quoted using what is commonly referred to as Negro slang. I just don't talk like that. Not all Negroes talk alike. I speak like a Nebraskan. There are expressions used in Harlem that I never heard, and there are expressions used in Nebraska that they never heard in Harlem.

Then there are the reporters who try to intimidate you, like the fellow who asked me what I thought about Gene Mauch saying the Cardinals would never win the pennant as long as Bob Gibson pitched for them. How do I know Mauch said that? Maybe the reporter was just trying to get me to react, to say something controversial about Mauch that could be put in big black headlines. I'm not easily intimidated.

A national magazine had a picture of me talking to George Crowe in the Cardinal clubhouse. They cropped the picture so that it showed nobody else in the clubhouse except George and myself and the caption said something like this: "Crowe and Gibson get together in the Cardinal clubhouse to discuss racial problems while the rest of the Cardinal team is on the field."

Now why would they want to write a thing like that? For one thing, we were not the only ones in the clubhouse. For another, we were not discussing racial problems. And for a third, if we were, how would the guy who wrote that caption know that we were?

Recently I had a verbal battle with the *Sporting News,* which blasted me in an editorial. Gibson, it said, "is No. 1 in just about every department you can name—except patience and affability." It said I refused to pose for a newspaper photographer and told him to "see my agent." That's what I mean about getting the facts. The incident occurred after I won the Corvette from *Sport* magazine as top performer in the World

Series. I didn't know he was a newspaper photographer. I just didn't want to have my picture taken for advertising purposes without checking with my agent to see if it was all right.

I have already talked about the constant errors involving my decision to give up basketball. I still read that it was because of my asthma attacks. Nobody has bothered to come and check with me on it.

Silly season for questions comes during the World Series. In this case the regular baseball writer is not to blame. Everybody covers the World Series—hundreds of reporters, some who might not cover a game all year.

One guy asked me after I had just won my third World Series game in 1967, if I was planning on playing the following season.

Another told me, after I had pitched a five-hit shutout, "You didn't have good stuff today."

"Oh no?" I said. "You should have had a bat."

I know I can be difficult for reporters at times, but some of them are pretty hard to take. They badger you. They expect you to give them your undivided attention and neglect your job so they can do theirs. They expect you to give them an hour of your time whenever they want it. They interview you in a crowd and whisper questions in your ear. And if you are not completely cooperative and friendly and attentive, they blast you. It's human nature, I guess, for people to expect perfection in everyone but themselves.

There are days when you just don't feel well and you would rather not be bothered. I don't usually like to talk to reporters before a game that I'm pitching. If I feel like talking to them I will, if I don't, I won't. If I get beat, I don't want to be bothered, but I'll talk to reporters because they have their job to do and it wasn't their fault I got beat.

Reporters are a necessary evil. They used to frighten me, but I think I've learned how to handle them. I don't let them agitate me, and if they ask me a question I don't want to answer, I tell them I don't want to answer it and let them write that. If I talk to a reporter and read that he has misquoted me or failed to get all the facts, I just don't talk to that reporter anymore.

Perhaps reporters have an excuse for their badgering and bad manners. They are trying to do their job. Fans have no excuse for their rudeness.

People come up and stop me on the street all the time to ask me all kinds of personal questions.

"How much money do you make?" they ask.

"How much money do you make?" I ask.

"Er, er, ah, uh," they say.

It's rude for somebody to ask you how much money you make. It's also rude for them to interrupt your dinner and start talking to you. Stan Musial is more patient. He stops, signs autographs, and talks with them. I am just not that way.

A lady came up to me while I was having dinner in a restaurant in Boston and asked me for my autograph. She had finished her meal and she put down her napkin and came over and interrupted my meal. It didn't matter to her that I was in the middle of cutting a piece of meat.

"Could I have your autograph?"

"Do you mind waiting until I am finished with my dinner?"

"I can't, I won't be here. I'm leaving."

I didn't sign.

I have no feeling one way or another about giving autographs. It wouldn't bother me if I never signed another one as long I live. But I don't flatly refuse to sign them. If I feel like it I will, and if I don't feel like it, I won't. You don't mind it when people are pleasant, but when they are rude and insistent, that annoys you, particularly if you are with friends enjoying yourself and they come and pester you.

After I broke my leg they took me on a stretcher from the Cardinal clubhouse to the hospital. While I was waiting in the doorway for the ambulance to arrive and in agony with the pain, some lady came up to me, shoved a piece of paper and a pencil in front of my face, and said rather matter-of-factly, "May I have your autograph?"

Sure you enjoy being recognized in public, but there's a limit and some people never know when to leave. Just suppose you were a garbage collector and every day about a hundred people stopped you and asked you how much garbage you collected that day and how much you expected to collect the next day. You've got to get pretty tired of that.

Once my wife and I were on an airplane, coming home after the World Series, and a man came up to me.

"Are you Bob Gibson?"

"Yes, I am."

"No, you aren't Bob Gibson, are you?"

"Yes, I am."

"Are you kidding me?"

"No, I'm not kidding you."

"You SOB, you cost me a lot of money in the World Series."

The fans in St. Louis are generally pretty good, but I was booed there once and it hurt me. I got knocked out in the first inning and as I came off the field I heard the boos. So I tipped my hat and they all cheered.

I felt bad enough as it was because ten minutes had passed and the Giants had pounded the stuffing out of me and scored 9 runs. This is the one time I had an emotion on the field. I felt hurt because I had been pitching there almost 10 years and did pretty well. Then they booed me. But that's how people are, I guess.

I care what people think about me. I care about the image I project. I like people to think I'm nice, that's all, but whatever image I project, that's it. I'm not going to go out of my way or bend over backward to have people think I'm nice. I want them to accept me as I am. I just hope that it is something good.

Since I am in the mood for getting things off my chest, it seems only fitting that another group should be included with reporters and fans. I mean umpires. You know what they say, umpires make mistakes just like everybody else, they just make more than anybody else . . . and when they die I know where they are all going.

Actually, I get along pretty good with umpires—except for the three times I was thrown out of a ballgame. I talk to them, fight with them, and laugh with them. Like reporters, they have a job to do and they are a necessary evil, and like ballplayers, they have their strengths and weaknesses.

Some will give you the low strike, some have a wide strike zone, others a narrow strike zone and some don't have any strike zone. You get to know them and the kind of strike zone they have, and it has a bearing on the way you pitch.

It's true that in the American League they give you the high strike and in the National League they give you the low strike. I would be more effective in the American League since I am a high-ball pitcher. I might get that high strike in the American League that I don't get in the National.

By the same token, if you throw the ball up there in the National League, they don't swing at it very often. In the American League hitters get used to jumping up after that high pitch. Hitters aren't stupid, but sometimes I think they believe they are smarter than they really are.

One of the best umpires, in my opinion, is Al Barlick, although he's tough on pitchers because he has a small strike zone. Al thinks I'm on him all the time and he's always looking to throw me out. One day he turned around, looked at our bench and yelled, "That's enough, Gibson."

"I wasn't even saying a word," I shouted back.

"Well, if you weren't, I'm just getting you for one time when you were."

Another time somebody was blistering him from our bench and he pulled off his mask and started toward our dugout.

I don't always like what I read in the papers, but I like reading in the bath—even the whirlpool.

"Is that Gibson over there?"

He looked into the dugout. No Gibson. I was in the club-house. So he put his mask back on and went back to work. A few minutes later I came up the dugout steps and McCarver yelled, "Hey, Al, you were looking for Gibson. Here he is."

He saw me coming up the steps from the clubhouse and he just looked over and we both laughed.

CHAPTER 14 *THE SPIRIT OF ST. LOUIS*

Three days before the start of the 1967 season we got a new player. Eddie Bressoud, a veteran infielder, came over from the Mets in exchange for Jerry Buchek, a young infielder.

"How do you feel about picking up an extra $10,000 this year?" I said as I shook hands with Ed and welcomed him to the Cardinals.

"I'd like that fine," he replied.

"Well just stick around here all year and you will."

This was not just idle talk. I went to St. Petersburg convinced we would win the 1967 National League pennant. It was not an opinion that was shared widely by baseball experts. They had pretty much agreed that the best we could do was finish sixth. Fortunately, the pennant is not decided in the newspapers in April.

There is always a tendency to overestimate the chances of the team you're with. Usually you see only the good things, the potential of a team, and it is impossible to take into account in April all that can happen during June, July, and August. By the same token, you never fool yourself. You know your team's weaknesses better than anybody else. You know its limitations. I took all this into consideration and I still felt we would win the pennant. So did Curt Flood. So did Tim McCarver.

We had finished sixth the year before, but we had improved tremendously although basically we had made only two changes. For one, we had Orlando Cepeda in spring training. For another, we had Roger Maris.

The reason the experts low-rated us, I believe, is because we had few big-name established winners on our pitching staff. But big names are not important, performance is. I knew our pitching would be better than most people thought it would be. Fellows like Steve Carlton and Nelson Briles were young and figured to improve, and we had a rookie in camp who looked like he would be a big help. Dick Hughes was the rookie, but he had been around baseball a long time. He was twenty-nine years old, knew how to pitch, and had great stuff. He came up at the end of 1966 to pitch in six games and looked great. During the winter I was talking with Loren Babe, who lives in Omaha and had seen Hughes in the International League when Loren managed in the Yankee farm system. "You guys have a pitcher in the minor leagues who can really throw," he said. He meant Hughes.

We had another change in the organization that spring, a new general manager. Stan Musial had agreed to take the job after Bob Howsam went to Cincinnati. At first I had reservations about Stan as a general manager. Great ballplayers rarely make good executives, but he proved to be a pleasant surprise and a pleasure to deal with. He knew the problems of the ballplayer and was sympathetic toward him.

Stan's assistant was Bob Stewart, a great guy who did a lot for the players and our wives. He helped us with our problems and did little things that made everyone more comfortable and made the season more enjoyable. He was very considerate of our problems, and we all appreciated it. He did more for the players in one year than had been done in my eight previous seasons with the club.

So I went to St. Pete for spring training convinced we would win the pennant. We were a club that had everything—pitching, speed, power, and defense. And we had something that does not show up in the box scores. I almost hesitate to mention it because it sounds high-schoolish, but that something else we had was team spirit.

I know we are professionals and that rah-rah stuff is not supposed to apply to us. I also know most players feel the same way about their club. And I know one more thing. I know that every player who came over from another team— Cepeda, Maris, Bressoud, Jack Lamabe—all of them said the same thing. They have never been with a team that had as much spirit as our team.

It is as difficult to explain as it is to understand. The Cardinal team has always been like that as long as I've been on it. All the guys seem to pull together. There are no cliques on the Cardinals. We have parties together, we go out together. I've gone out with Bob Skinner when he was on the team and I go out with Dal Maxvill a lot. We go to dinner or out on the town in San Francisco or Chicago or Los Angeles. We don't have three separate groups like some clubs, where the Negro guys stay together, the Spanish guys stay together, and the white guys stay together.

If a guy doesn't like you on the Cardinals you know it. We don't keep it inside, we let it out in the open and clear the air.

I tell you these things and I know a lot of people say, "Aw, hogwash," but it's true. I think the reason it's true—and I'm going to violate my code and be a little prejudiced here—is that the Negro ballplayers that have been on the Cardinal club, such as Bill White, George Crowe, Curt Flood, myself, have always demanded a certain amount of respect. We didn't go for all that old stuff, going in the back and telling those nasty colored jokes. And all this prejudice stuff, we didn't tolerate it, and if we heard it, we let everybody know right then that we didn't care for it. If you don't like me as a Negro, then just don't bother with me. That's the way it is on the Cardinal ballclub.

In spring training recently one of the young kids on our club was talking about Mike Epstein and he used the expression "Superjew."

"Why do you call him that?" I asked.

"Everybody does," he said.

Well, to me that didn't make it right, and I chewed him up one side and down the other about it.

There is a player in our league who is supposed to either have invented or endorsed a nickname for himself—Supernigger—and I want to tell you I don't like it either way. I don't believe in joking around like that. I don't tell colored jokes and I don't stand for others telling them.

Charline was in spring training in 1965 and she was talking with several of the other wives and this one girl, a white wife of one of our younger players, said something about me, referring to me as "Supernigger." She said it three or four times, but my wife didn't say anything. This girl was young and naïve and Charline didn't want to embarrass her, but she called her aside later and asked her why she used that expression.

"Well, that's what he calls himself, isn't it?" she said.

"No, he doesn't," Charline said simply and calmly. "He never would and I strongly advise you not to either."

I can be sitting in a movie and I hear that word and the perspiration just starts rolling down. "Nigger." It just turns me over. I remember seeing that show Sammy Davis was in, "Golden Boy," and they used that word several times and it turned me over. I started perspiring. It's just a reflex action.

I know Dick Gregory uses the word a lot. And makes fun of it. And sells books with it. I don't condemn that and I don't condone it. I don't know Dick Gregory personally, so I cannot have an opinion of him, but I know he goes out risking his life and spending a lot of money for this cause, but he's not the only one risking his life and spending his money. He's doing things he doesn't have to do for progress and I respect

I keep a guitar in my locker. Stan Musial (left) and Al Jackson don't seem to mind a few sour notes. *UPI* him for it, but he's doing them because he wants to do them, so if he wants to use that word, that's his business, not mine. But I still don't like it.

As far as deploring hypocrisy, I don't deplore it all that much. You can say whatever you want to say as long as I don't hear it. I just want to be shown respect as a human being, that's all.

Now I've wandered away from my original point, which is simply that on the Cardinal ball club the Negro players have demanded and earned respect from the other players and there is mutual respect, whites for Negroes, Negroes for Latins, Latins for whites, Negroes for whites. There is harmony. Togetherness. And that's what I mean by spirit and why I feel the Cardinals get a little more out of their players than most other teams. This may not win pennants, but it helps.

Back in 1964 we got a lot of national publicity because we began to wear rubber horror masks. It began in 1963, but it didn't get national attention until we won the pennant in 1964. We had all seen a horror movie on the Late Late Show in Milwaukee and the next day we went out and bought those masks. Ray Sadecki had a Wolf Man mask. Tim McCarver was the Hunchback of Notre Dame. I was Franken-stein. Another player was somebody else.

We'd wear them on airplanes and scare the stewardesses and we'd wear them on the bus going to the ball park and we'd stick our heads out the window and get a double-take from passers-by. It sounds childish but it was fun, and it was the kind of thing that kept us together and gave us camara-derie. It helped make us more like a fraternity than a baseball team and was all part of the spirit we had on the club. We still have it even though the mask bit stopped after Sadecki was traded to the Giants.

McCarver and I have reputations for being agitators, but Lou Brock is kind of an agitator too, in a quiet way. He's the kind of guy who pulls a practical joke and makes it look like somebody else did it. He'll take record albums out of my locker when I am not looking and stick them in Cepeda's locker, and then I will come in and accuse Cepeda of stealing them. And poor Orlando will look bewildered while Lou is off in the corner of the room somewhere laughing his head off.

Lou likes to kid, and his primary target is Cepeda. He agitates him all the time. Orlando will get mad and say, "That Brock makes me so mad I'm going to go out and get four hits today."

Cepeda is a big, good-natured guy, almost like a kid sometimes. When he was with the Giants, I used to play winter ball with him in Puerto Rico. He was such a friendly guy, and somebody told me the way to get on him was to call him Cepeda, not Orlando.

"Why you call me Cepeda?" he would pout. "You mad at me?"

Curt Flood is a quiet guy, but he has a quick, sharp sense of humor. He has so much talent he frightens you. He paints, plays the ukelele, and sometimes I think he could do anything he puts his mind to. He often seems preoccupied, but he is a real baseball fan, worse than some of the people in the bleachers.

When he is playing he is quiet, but on a day when he does not play, he can't sit still in the dugout. He's like a cheerleader, yelling, clapping his hands, cheering all the time. If I'm sitting next to him, I keep jabbing him, trying to get him to keep quiet.

"For crying out loud," I tell him, "if you want to make so much noise, why don't you buy a ticket and get up in the stands."

Joe Hoerner, one of our young pitchers, likes to play practical jokes. He'll wait until you bend down to tie your shoelace, then he'll pounce on top of you and the next thing you know there are eight guys jumping on you. Red Schoendienst doesn't like that very much.

Like most baseball teams, the Cardinals are loaded down with unusual and descriptive nicknames which the players tag on each other. They call me "Hoot." Cepeda is "Cha-Cha." Maxvill is "Bonesy" because he's so skinny. Larry Jaster is "Creeper" because he kind of creeps around very quietly. Maris is "Rajah."

Julian Javier is "The Phantom" because he makes the double play so quickly and gets out of the way of the runner so fast, he's like a phantom. Runners have been trying to get to him and dump him for ten years and they haven't done it yet.

I named Dick Hughes "The Sniper." We were in Atlanta and he bought a hunting rifle with a scope and he would look out his hotel room window and test the scope by lining people up in the sight.

Ray Washburn answers to the name "Deadbody." He never walks faster than a snail. Joe Schultz, one of our coaches, calls McCarver "Doggie" because he looks like a dog. Same for Hoerner, who we call "Bulldog." Ron Willis, another of our young pitchers, is "Gomer" or "Andy Gump" because he has a weak chin.

Mike Shannon is the "Moon Man" and if you ever talked with him, you'd know why. He'll talk for fifteen minutes and when he's through you'll go away scratching your head and wondering what he said. He may start a conversation about baseball and end up with insurance after going through forty-five other topics. You still don't know what he said.

We have this diathermy machine in the clubhouse with lights always blinking on and off. When it's on and the lights are going crazy, Flood will look at it and say, "There goes the machine talking to the Moon Man again."

Sure it's all silly stuff, but it's a long season and it helps ease the tension of a tight pennant race or a depressing losing streak. You're twenty-five guys and you're all together from February to October. You spend more time with each other than you do with your own families. You room together, eat together, travel together, go out together. You share each others' hopes and promises, joys and sorrows, successes and failures. You're almost totally dependent on one another. And if twenty-five guys can be happy together and enjoy each other's company and have mutual trust, respect, and understanding, you're on your way to having a successful baseball team.

CHAPTER 15 *THE RIGHT PITCH*

We jumped them right from the start. The 1967 season was only a week old and we let them know, right away, that the Cardinals were a team that would bear watching. We played six games and won them all. We beat Juan Marichal twice in that first week.

Talk about good starts. We opened in St. Louis on Tuesday, April 11, and with 38,117 fans cheering us on, we took the field for the first time.

In the first inning I struck out Ken Henderson. I struck out Jesus Alou. I struck out Willie Mays.

In the second inning I struck out Willie McCovey. I struck out Jim Ray Hart. It was a pretty good way to start a new season I thought, but how long could this possibly last? The sixth batter, Tom Haller, ended it by flying out. I finished with 13 strikeouts and a 6–0, five-hit victory. I was particularly pleased because the Giants beat me three out of three in 1966.

I settled another old score eleven days later when I beat the Dodgers, 3–1, on a five-hitter, my first victory over them after 6-straight defeats. It was my third victory in three games. I am usually a notoriously slow starter. I begin picking up in the second half of the season. The way I started out gave me encouragement that this would be my best year. In the last

131

four seasons I had won 18, 19, 20, and 21 games. I was hoping to keep the arithmetic progression and make it 22 in 1967—although I would settle for more.

There were, I believe, three reasons for my improvement as a pitcher. The first was experience and the second was control, although, in a sense, these two go together. The third was perfecting my curve ball, which gave me another effective pitch to go with my slider and two fast balls—the one that sails and the one that sinks.

Basically I am a fast-ball pitcher and a high-ball pitcher. My best pitch is the fast ball that sails and rides away from a right-handed batter. That's the pitch with which I get most of my strikeouts. When I'm not striking them out, they're popping it up. My ball moves. If it doesn't move, I get killed. If it's moving, I'm going to be all right.

The key to pitching success is control. I don't mean whether or not you walk a lot of batters, I mean getting the ball in the strike zone. Not right over the middle, but somewhere near the area you're trying to hit. If you are close to that area and you have good stuff on the ball, you're going to be all right.

Against Pittsburgh a couple of years ago I was just rearing back and throwing the ball without paying too much attention to where it was going. I really had good stuff. I was throwing hard. But the harder I threw, the harder they hit it. They clipped me for 6 runs in the second inning, which shows that you can throw too hard and get hurt by it.

I know that if I've got my control and my good stuff, I can beat any team I pitch against. If I don't have my good stuff or if I'm missing my spots, I'm going to struggle and probably get beat. It's as simple as that. No matter who I pitch against I always feel completely confident I'm going to win. I think that in order to be successful, that's the way you have to feel.

You never can tell in advance whether you're going to have good stuff. You might think you have good stuff warming up in the bullpen, then when you get in the game you find your stuff is not good at all.

Usually, in the first two innings I can barely tell how I'm throwing. So I'll ask McCarver and he'll say, "You're throwing good." Or he might say, "You're not throwing so good." Then I'll go out and try a little harder. On days when I have exceptionally good stuff, I can tell from the very first pitch.

Some days you throw harder than others. I don't know why. I don't think anybody knows. I've pitched some very good games on days when I didn't eat well and didn't sleep well the night before. And I've been knocked out early after having a good meal and a good night's rest. There is just no answer.

The slider is my second-best pitch. I generally rely pretty much on the hard stuff—fast ball and slider—and that's interesting because I don't throw as hard as I used to four or five years ago, yet I'm a better pitcher now than I was then. The reason is simple. Control, experience, and knowing how to pitch.

I know I don't throw as hard as I did formerly. Now when I grip it with the seams I can make it sink every time. Before I couldn't. So I know I'm not throwing as hard, because the harder you throw the less your ball will move. There is not as much time for it to break. Also, if a ball has a greater velocity, the air currents will have less effect on it. I have compensated for my loss of speed with better control and more movement.

Nobody has ever measured how hard I throw, but as a gauge I would say I throw as hard as Sandy Koufax did. I don't throw as hard as Jim Maloney of the Cincinnati Reds. Nobody throws as hard as Maloney in my opinion. He's the only guy who can simply overpower you. You know he's going to throw the fast ball, you set for it, but you still can't catch up with it.

I am not being boastful when I say I throw as hard as Koufax threw. Sandy was a great pitcher, but surprisingly, although he threw hard, it was not his fastball that made him great. I didn't see him in his earlier days. He probably overpowered you then, but it wasn't until he learned control that he became a big winner. And by then he probably had lost some zip off his fast ball. Sandy's greatest assets were his terrific curve ball and great control. He could throw that curve ball for strikes anytime he wanted. And he'd throw it down around your knees, making it an impossible pitch to hit. His fast ball would jump as it reached the plate. I still contend you couldn't hit him if you stood deep in the batter's box, which is an unorthodox theory. Most hitters like to stand deep so they can wait on the ball awhile longer. With Sandy that was a mistake. If you stood up in the box, you could get the fast ball before it hopped and the curve ball before it completed its arc.

I told this to one of our young infielders, Ed Spiezio, when he was scheduled to start against Koufax one day.

He tried it and he hit the ball hard three times. He didn't get a base hit, but he hit three line drives, what ballplayers call "ropes." He came back and told me, "You know, Hoot, that really worked."

I've been telling those guys that. They stand back there and he throws the fast ball by them . . . whoosh. One day I hit against him and used my theory. I got two hits. The whole team only got four.

Juan Marichal of the Giants has probably the best control and the best assortment of pitches in the game today. He doesn't throw as hard as a lot of pitchers, but again, he is proof that control is the key to a pitcher's success. He throws several different curve balls all at various speeds. But his biggest asset is that he can throw any one of his wide assortment of pitches just about anywhere he wants, any time he wants.

Maloney throws harder than anybody and Bob Veale of the Pittsburgh Pirates is not far behind, but both have control trouble, and that is their biggest problem.

Jim Bunning of the Pirates is a pitcher who relies on his fast ball at an age when most pitchers are either retired or getting by with soft stuff. Bunning has great control too. Also a great fast ball and good curve ball. He's tough. A good pitcher, no ifs, ands, or buts about it.

I grip the ball across the seams to throw the fast ball that sails.
Bob Brown

Two views of my grip for the fast ball that sinks. It's held with the seams. *Bob Brown*

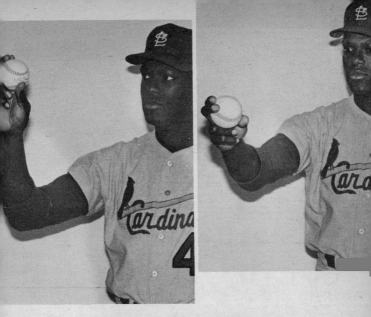

I throw the slider with a stiff wrist and I try to cut through the middle of the ball with my fingers. *Bob Brown*

I hold my curve ball with the seams and throw it in a downward motion with a loose wrist. *Bob Brown*

The follow-through is very important. The idea is to get into position quickly to field the ball. *UPI*

The Phillies' Chris Short has a good fast ball and a good, hard slider.

For a youngster, the Reds' Gary Nolan has exceptional control and a good breaking ball to go with a strong fast ball.

Don Drysdale of the Dodgers can be as tough as anybody. Like me, he also throws two different fast balls. He's particularly tough against right-handed batters because he's so tall and he comes at you sidearm.

I admire Larry Jackson of the Phils because he knows how to pitch, and my buddy Al Jackson of the Mets is as tough as they come when he keeps the ball low. He's a sinker-ball pitcher, and if he comes up he gets hurt.

In the brief time I saw Jim Lonborg of the Boston Red Sox, he showed me good control and a good slider, but I didn't think he was overpowering.

On our club Dick Hughes has a high hard one similar to the fast ball I throw that sails. That's his best pitch. He and I are about the only pitchers on the Cardinals who can get away with throwing a high fast ball. Nelson Briles has two basic pitches, a fast ball that sails into a right-handed hitter and away from a left-handed hitter, and a curve ball, but no slider. Young Steve Carlton, a lefthander, has one of the best curve balls in the league.

All the fellows I mentioned are good pitchers and could beat any team on any given day. Nobody makes a living hitting against them or would enjoy a steady diet of hitting against them. Hitters have a way of letting you know they respect you that makes pitchers mad, because the guy who complains about having to face you is the guy that beats you.

Hitters tell me, "Boy, I sure don't want to hit against you, Gibson." It's not that they are afraid or are giving up, because they beat you anyway. Nobody liked hitting against Koufax, but he didn't win all his games . . . although he didn't lose many. Maybe it's psychological warfare on their part. Willie Mays is always asking me, "When are you pitching, Gibson?" Then he goes out and knocks my brains out.

Admittedly I go into most games planning to rely on the fast ball and slider, but my curve has improved in recent years. You just can't go out there and throw hard every four days. There are some games you don't have the hard one and you try to get by with curve balls and sliders on days like that. I've reached the point where I can throw my curve ball for strikes consistently and I have games—though not many— where I will throw 50 percent curve balls and sliders. Usually I will not throw a curve ball after the sixth inning. When you're tired, that's when a curve ball is dangerous. You're not pulling down as hard on it as you should and it hangs. A hanging curve is the pitch that is hit for a home run.

I would discourage youngsters of sandlot age from throwing curve balls until their arms are mature enough to stand the strain. It depends on a boy's physical structure. It's all right for a big, strong kid, but dangerous for a frail boy. I would strongly discourage any boy from throwing curve balls until he is seventeen or eighteen. He should throw fast balls and experiment with his grip to see how he can get it to move best. Another thing youngsters should remember is to keep the ball well hidden in the glove to avoid tipping pitches.

I'll throw an occasional changeup, but it's not a good one. For the past few years I've been working on a knuckle ball as insurance against the day when I might not be able to get by with hard stuff and I'll have to go to something else. I throw it on the sidelines or in the bullpen on a day when I'm pitching. I'll usually make my last two or three warmup pitches knuckleballs. I haven't thrown it in a game yet. I have not perfected it to the point where I can control it and know where it's going. I'll continue to work on it until I have enough confidence that I can get it over the plate. Then I'll throw it in a game. I don't believe in going into a game with a pitch I have not developed.

A good knuckleball pitcher like Hoyt Wilhelm doesn't know how much it is going to break all the time, but he has a pretty good idea where it's going each time.

I believe you have to go to any pitch you can master, and I am preparing for that day, particularly since the kids they keep bringing up throw harder and harder. I think all athletes are better—pitchers, hitters, basketball players, football players. They start much younger than they used to. They're bigger, stronger, have better diets, better coaching. Records are constantly being broken, so they must be better. In baseball the gloves are bigger, so fielding has improved, more home runs are being hit than ever before, and the pitchers have better control and a greater variety of pitches.

But there will always be room for the veteran pitcher with control, even if he cannot throw hard. So I will try anything to stay around. Even the spit ball.

I've thrown the spitter . . . not often, but I've thrown it. Maybe a dozen times in my career. I'll throw it every once in a while just to see what happens. Not in a tough situation, because I don't have complete control over it. Rules or no rules, pitchers are going to throw spitters. It's a matter of survival. You don't have to get moisture from your mouth to throw it. You can get it from the perspiration off your wrists, from the back of your neck, off your brow.

Some pitchers throw the spitter all the time. Lew Burdette threw one. I played with him and I know he did. The pitchers on your own team, you know about. The others you can only guess. But you have a pretty good idea because of the way the ball reacts to moisture. It comes up to the plate and drops 6 or 7 inches like the bottom fell out. Nothing does that but a spit ball.

I can think of about ten pitchers who throw it, and I guess I can't blame them. The hitters have enough of an advantage as it is, so some pitchers try to minimize the advantage by throwing the spitter. Hitters get mad when you throw one. They use 40-ounce bats, 38-inches long, but they complain if you throw a spit ball.

The kind of pitcher I am, with the kind of stuff I throw,

people have a tendency to believe I don't pitch, I just throw. For years I have tried to destroy the notion that I am not a thinking pitcher. I just don't believe you can be a good pitcher without thinking. I don't care who you are. Your stuff is never that good. I don't care how hard you throw, if you throw that ball over the middle of the plate somebody is going to knock the stuff out of it.

Take Koufax. People think he just reared back and fired the ball. Oh no! He'd rear back and hit the corner. He rarely threw a ball over the middle of the plate. And he rarely threw it inside, except when he wanted to get you back off that plate, and then he'd come back and hit that outside corner where you couldn't reach it.

Just because a guy throws hard does not mean he doesn't think. Maloney, for example. He has an idea of what he wants to do. His control is not that good, so he might not get the ball where he wants it, but he has an idea. It's nice to know people think you have good enough stuff that you don't have to think, but it's not true. The pitcher who doesn't think is the pitcher who doesn't win.

Howie Pollett, who used to be the Cardinals' pitching coach, once said he thought I could win 30 games. I don't think anybody will ever win 30 games again. You don't get to stay in games long enough. It's not like the old days when a pitcher started and went all the way. He'd win, 10–9, or 8–7. We're living in an age of specialization in everything, and that's particularly true in baseball. Just as soon as you give up a couple of runs, in comes a relief pitcher. Also the schedule is so tight you don't get to make enough starts to win 30. I've never had 40 starts in a season and only once did I have more than 35.

Nor do I think I will ever pitch a no-hitter. I make too many mistakes to pitch a no-hitter. Somewhere along the way I make a mistake and somebody is going to capitalize on it. The closest I ever came to pitching a no-hitter was 8 2/3 innings in the minor leagues. I'd like to have one, sure, but my heart is not going to break if I don't get one.

I enjoy pitching. What I don't enjoy is not pitching. That is, I hate the three or four days between starts, but I love it the day I'm pitching. I like to be active and I like to hit. Most pitchers like to hit. I'm considered a pretty good hitter—good enough to be used as a pinch-hitter occasionally—but not as good as I could be. The reason is pitchers don't get enough batting practice. They're too busy running in the outfield and shagging flies and pitching batting practice. That's no fun.

If I had it to do over again, I'd be an everyday ballplayer. Some guys have all the fun.

CHAPTER 16 *BRUSHBACK*

One of the most valuable weapons at a pitcher's command is the brushback pitch. First let me clear something up. A brushback pitch is not to be confused with a deliberate knockdown. There is a difference. A world of a difference.

A deliberate knockdown is when you throw a ball at a hitter's head. You want to knock him down, maybe even hit him. It's a pouting gesture. A guy has been wearing you out and you want to show him you're in the ballgame too. You're not going to stand for that stuff. So you throw the ball at his head. Now you know that's no mistake, because there's no way you can miss the plate that far.

I will never knock a hitter down just because he hits me hard. If he hits a home run off me it's because I made a mistake. It's my fault, not his. If I make a mistake why should I pout and take it out on the hitter? If I make a good pitch, nine times out of ten I'm going to get him out.

The only time I will knock a guy down is if my men are getting knocked down. The manager will instruct you to get even, but he doesn't have to tell me. I'm going to get somebody on the other team. That's the only way I can protect the guys I play with. They're out there trying to help me earn my living.

When I knock a batter down I'm telling the other team they're not going to hit my men and get away with it. I'm not intending to hit him. I can hit him if I want to, that's not difficult. I usually like to knock down the pitcher who started it, but sometimes you have to throw at the first batter in the inning to stop it right away. That usually puts an end to the throwing—but not always.

On July 3, 1967, a throwing match resulted in the biggest fight I have ever seen on a field. A real knock-down and drag-out that lasted about forty minutes. Everytime it seemed to cool off, it would break out again someplace else. Naturally, it all started with someone getting hit.

We were playing the Cincinnati Reds in St. Louis. We had scored 7 runs in the first inning, which is enough to make any team mad. Julian Javier was knocked down by Don Nottebart in the third inning. Lou Brock was hit in the fourth. That did it. We had been getting hit a lot all season—especially Lou—and since I was pitching, it was my obligation to protect my teammates.

Tony Perez led off the fifth inning. My first pitch sailed over his head. Mission accomplished. I figured that would end it and I went back to pitching my game. Perez popped up, and as he passed me he said something.

I don't know what he said. You never know. There are 50,000 people yelling and somebody gets on you and you can't hear it, but you know he's getting on you. So you say something back.

"Here I am," I said, "come and get me."

Perez accepted the invitation. He started for the mound, but was interrupted by Orlando Cepeda, a peacemaker. All of a sudden here comes Bob Lee out of the Cincinnati bullpen, yelling and screaming and looking for Cepeda. He found him. Cha-Cha hit him two left hooks and a right cross and the next thing you knew both dugouts had emptied and there were fights all over the place. I ended up in the Cincinnati dugout

The brushback has got to cause arguments. Johnny Keane and Tim McCarver are doing the talking here.   *Ken Regan*

with three guys on top of me, beating me on the head. I hit about six or seven players. I didn't even know who they were, I was just swinging. They might have been my own teammates who had come to help me. It was pretty wild out there, but there was no more throwing the rest of the series.

That doesn't happen often.

A brushback pitch, on the other hand, is more common. It's part of a pitcher's strategy. A brushback has its place in baseball. Most people misinterpret its purpose. A brushback is not to scare a hitter or to hit him. It's to make him think.

Normally, it's thrown after a batter gets to leaning out over the plate. If you pitch a guy outside consistently he's going to start leaning. He knows you're going out there and he's going to kill you. So you come in and knock him back off that plate. Now you've got him thinking, "I better not go out there too far," and then you come back with a pitch on the outside corner. The idea is to get him reaching for the ball. When he's reaching, he's not going to hit it good.

One time I was pitching against the Dodgers in the Los Angeles Coliseum, which had a very short left-field fence. I pitched away to Duke Snider because he was a good pull hitter and he reached out and poked it over the left-field fence. The next time he came up, I was still going to pitch him outside. I noticed he began to edge out there after it, so I threw the next pitch tight to brush him back away from the plate. But he was expecting the ball away and he was still leaning and the ball hit him and broke his elbow.

I saw Duke after the game. His arm was in a cast. "I really got it good that time," he said.

I didn't apologize to him. What's the sense in saying I was sorry. He knew I was sorry. He knew I wasn't throwing at him. I was just trying to move him away from the plate, trying to get him to think and not take things for granted up there.

Now that's the way I see the Negro riots we're having in this country, as a brushback pitch. Their intention, like the brushback pitch, is to get people to think and not to get complacent and take things for granted. Negroes have been mistreated for years. They are getting tired of being mistreated, misused, and misunderstood, and the only way they can rebel is to stage riots.

If you're getting pushed around, if they're knocking you all around the lot, you're going to protect yourself. You're going to brush him back from the plate. You're going to riot and get him to think a little. Blowing up places and rioting are, in my opinion, just like a brushback pitch.

The reason for the riots is to point out to people that these things are going on and they should be changed, something should be done. The white man sits back expecting the Negro to fail. The Negro can succeed. All he needs is a little help like everybody else has had.

I don't want to see anybody get hurt or anybody's property destroyed, but how are you going to get people to think? People get hurt, but it has to happen. That's the way the world is. People fight, they get things accomplished, they have peace for a while, then they fight again. This country's history is filled with violence. Whatever freedom we have was achieved because of violence, and to achieve it somebody had to get hurt.

In a way this is no different from colonial Americans and their fight for independence against England. They wanted to be recognized and this was the only way they could do it. By fighting. If somebody won't listen to you and you know you have a right to a certain thing, what else are going to do?

If I'm a Negro and you're a white man and I've been trying to get to see you for ten years and I get nowhere, I have to begin to wonder how long this is going to go on. Now I've got to make you notice me. I've been trying to talk to you for ten years and you haven't noticed me. So I'll go and kick your door down and then you'll notice me.

"Why did you kick my door down?" you'll ask.

"Because I've been trying to get in to see you for ten years."

So now we'll talk over our problems. A lot of places hire Negroes just so somebody won't knock their door down, and that's an accomplishment. Maybe the institution of the house Negro—for showcase only—is a poor beginning. The boss' Negro secretary is becoming more common around the country, even though it may be only for show. But pretty soon somebody's going to come in and see her there and he's going to go back home and get to thinking maybe he'll hire a Negro too. Not just to sit out front, but to do some real work. And pretty soon he's going to find out she's just as valuable to him as any other employee.

Things are getting better, but they're not getting better fast enough. I'll tell you one way they'd get better faster in Omaha —if they start blowing up downtown Omaha instead of their own homes in the ghetto.

You hear a great deal about Black Power. It's just a phrase but a lot of people have different ideas about what it means. I think the average white person thinks when you say Black Power that the Negroes are trying to take over the world. I don't think that's the idea at all. I think the idea is to show that the Negro does have some power and when he votes his vote is just as important as anybody else's. And that the Negro is looking for equality and the opportunity to advance himself just like everybody else.

One thing that disturbs me is when they refer to Rap Brown and Stokely Carmichael as Negro leaders. They never refer to Robert Shelton, head of the Ku Klux Klan, as a white leader. Why does a Negro need a leader? We're not sheep. I'm a Negro but my leader is the President of the United States, the same as everybody else's.

There was an orderly demonstration in Omaha a few years ago when 10,000 Negroes turned out to march in front of City Hall to try to get a fair-housing ordinance passed. Charline wanted to go and take the children. I was against it. I was afraid the children would get hurt. But Charline felt strongly about it, so I let her go. I sat in the car and watched, and it was a peaceful demonstration. Nobody got hurt. But I wouldn't march. I'm afraid if I'm marching down the street and somebody throws something or spits at me, I'm going to step right out of line and punch him. I have enough sense to try to keep away from the things that might make me violent. But rioting has its place. I don't want to see anybody get hurt, but if somebody asks me bluntly, "Are you glad there are riots?" I'd have to be equally blunt and answer, "Yes."

I've had an awful lot of opportunities lately and I know why. The opportunities are getting better and not because I'm playing baseball any better. Not that much better anyway. It's got to be the result of all that's been going on.

I must admit I'm participating in those riots vicariously. Not rooting for anybody to get hurt. I couldn't live with that thought. But I'm in there in spirit just like so many other Negroes who have been less fortunate than I.

After the 1967 World Series I got a letter from a Mr. Miller congratulating me on my season and on the fine example I was setting for the youth of Omaha.

"You see," he wrote, "with a lot of hard work you can get somewhere in the world. You don't have to stage riots and demonstrations."

Here's a well-meaning man who was still not aware of the fact, or did not grasp the seriousness of the fact, that Negroes have problems that cannot be solved simply by hard work. He was using me as an example. Unfortunately, everybody can't play baseball. It proved to me that so many well-meaning people are just plain unaware of the problems that the Negro has to overcome in the ghetto. He meant well, but he just did not understand. People say they understand the problem, but they don't understand it, because they are not Negroes. They can sympathize, but they can't understand. Maybe one day they will.

CHAPTER 17 *THE HITTERS*

Roberto Clemente stood at bat looking mean and menacing. His body was loose and wiry, like a spring ready to uncoil. I got ahead of him, 1 ball, 2 strikes, and now it began, the classic cat-and-mouse duel of pitcher against batter.

This is the kind of challenge you enjoy, trying to outthink the hitter. There are no secrets, no surprises. You know him and he knows you. You've pitched against him maybe 200 times. Nothing changes that much. What you try to do is stay one step ahead of him, get him expecting a different pitch in a different spot, get him off balance, get him leaning or reaching for the ball. In the final analysis what it comes down to is making a good pitch, hitting the spot. If I hit my spot, I'm going to get him out. If I don't, chances are he's going to hit it.

You can get almost anybody out by throwing to a certain spot. But you can't hit that spot all the time. You're going to make mistakes, and that's why guys bat .300.

Tim McCarver, my catcher, signaled for a fast ball away. I shook him off. Let me digress here and explain our system of signs. I have four basic pitches—fast ball, curve ball, slider, and change of pace. Tim will stick out one finger for the fast ball, two for the curve, three for the slider, four for the change. At the same time he will indicate where he wants the

Ken Regan

pitch by waving his fingers either to the left or right. First he puts down the number of fingers, then he waves.

In the case of the fast ball, the wave tells me which fast ball he wants. He'll put down one finger and wave to the right. That tells me he wants the fast fall that sails and rides away from a right-handed batter. If he puts down one finger and waves to the left, he wants the fast ball that sinks and rides away from a left-handed hitter.

I shake him off by a prearranged indicator. We might start out in the first inning agreeing that if I want to shake him off I'll wipe my glove along my uniform. That might mean add one number. That is, if he has put down two fingers for the curve ball and I wipe, then he adds one and puts down three fingers—the slider.

There are any number of variations I can use for shaking him off. One inning, wiping might mean add, the next inning it might mean subtract. Or you can wipe with a downward motion to add and with an upward motion to subtract. Or you can wipe below your belt to add and above your belt to subtract. All of these, of course, can be reversed to keep the opposition from picking up your indicator.

When you work with a catcher long enough, the two of you get to thinking together. Tim and I rarely disagree on what pitch to throw, but there are times when we do. In any case, I'll usually throw what I want to throw. I'm pitching the game. If I lose, I get the blame, not the catcher.

In some cases, where there is a veteran catcher, the manager will insist on the catcher calling the game. In my case, I've been around longer than Tim, so I call my own game.

I knew what I wanted to do with Clemente. I wanted to pitch him away because I think he hits the inside pitch better than he does the outside pitch. He's one of those hitters you have to move the ball around on. He'll hit the inside pitch to the opposite field better than anybody else around.

Because my best pitches are the fast ball that rides away from a right-handed hitter and the slider, lefthanders are tougher for me than righthanders. The two hitters who give me the most trouble—naturally they're left-handed—are Willie Davis and Ron Fairly of the Dodgers. I try to pitch Davis up and in. He'll chase a bad ball up. Somehow I always get the fast ball down and in and it seems that every time I look around he's standing on second base with a double. I think I make more mistakes against him than any other hitter in the league, and I never seem to get away with a mistake against him.

I don't have to make a mistake against Fairly. Whatever I throw, he just hits it, I don't care what it is. And always when somebody's on base. The guy's just a pretty good hitter. Fairly likes to talk to you a lot, especially when he's just had two or three hits. One day I was on first base and he came over and started a conversation.

"Boy, you've got good stuff," he said. "I don't know why you don't win 20 every year."

Usually I never answer him, but this day I did. "Oh, bull," I said. "You've always got something to say about nothing." He hasn't talked to me since.

I don't like to talk to players on other teams. I'm supposed to be out there trying to beat them. About the only players I'll talk to are the ones I used to play with—Bill White, Al Jackson, Ray Sadecki. I visited Willie Mays at his home in San Francisco once, but that was because I was with White and he and Willie were close friends from having played together with the Giants.

Another time the Giants were playing in St. Louis and Bill had Willie and me out to his house for dinner. Before dinner, we sat down to watch some sporting event on television and I took out my glasses, which I wear when I read, when I drive, when I watch television. Just about the only time I don't wear my glasses is when I'm pitching.

Mays looked at me with a surprised expression on his face. "You wear glasses?" he asked.

"Sure," I said.

"Don't you wear them when you pitch?"

"No," I replied.

"You crazy?" he squealed. "You're going to kill somebody."

There are a few exceptions, but ordinarily I don't want to be bothered with a guy I'm trying to beat. Lots of players do. They'll get together for dinner after a game. That's all right if they want to do it. I don't.

Probably the toughest lineup in the league is the Atlanta Braves'. Every one of them can hurt you, right down the line. Of course you start with Hank Aaron, who is one of the best hitters in the game. Aaron is a great fast-ball hitter, but not a very good breaking-ball hitter, so you try to throw him good curve balls and sliders.

Joe Torre: I don't have a lot of trouble with Joe. I pitch him inside. He likes to get his arms out away from his body, so I keep the ball in on him. He knows I'm coming in and you can see him snap around sometimes. If you get a good pitch in there with good stuff on it, you can get him out.

Rico Carty: I don't have much trouble with Rico. I pitch him breaking balls away.

Clete Boyer: An exceptionally good fast-ball hitter. I pitch him breaking balls away and try not to give him too many fast balls to hit.

Felipe Alou: A great hitter, in my opinion much better than his brother Matty, even if he doesn't hit for as high an average. When Felipe gets a hit, it's usually a line drive. He doesn't get too many cheap hits.

When I talk about how I get hitters out, let me emphasize that what works for me may not work for some other pitcher, just as what works for him may not work for me. You have to know your own ability, your own strengths and weaknesses. That's why I have little faith in scouting reports. Hank Aaron may not be a good breaking-ball hitter, but if you don't have a good breaking ball, he's going to hit it. In most cases, the best thing to do is match your strength against the hitter's strength. You have to challenge him.

I'm a high-ball pitcher. That doesn't mean I can't pitch low, but I'm more effective high. If a hitter is a good high-ball hitter, what do I do? I try to pitch him low because I have pretty good stuff low. If I didn't I would pitch him high, match my strength against his, and see who comes out on top. If I don't have a good breaking ball on a particular day, I don't dare throw it to Aaron. Even though he's a good fast-ball hitter, I have to throw him fast balls and take my chances.

Many hitters hit the breaking ball better than the fast ball. Willie Mays is one. I'll throw him a breaking ball, but I'll try not to make it too good. I'll throw him more fast balls. He will chase the high fast ball out of the strike zone, and you can get him out with a bad pitch. Willie was always a better breaking-ball hitter, even when he was younger. Now it's especially true because he's older and his reflexes have slowed a little . . . but only a little. He's still a tough hitter. I'm afraid he's going to be around four or five more years.

Mays has a habit of bailing out—pulling away from a pitch. That may look like a flaw, but it really isn't. Once the pitcher releases the ball, Willie comes back in and that's not bailing out at all. He's set to hit the pitch when it gets there. Most hitters can't reset like that, but Willie's reflexes are so good, he can do it.

Cepeda is also a better breaking-ball hitter than he is a fast-ball hitter. So is Tim McCarver. I'm not giving away any secrets, everybody knows this. You still have to make a good pitch.

Another good breaking-ball hitter is Ron Santo of the Cubs. He's just a good hitter, period, but I think he hits the breaking ball better because he's got good power to the opposite field. He hits the ball away from him and the breaking ball is usually away. I try to pitch him fast balls inside. You can get him out keeping the ball in on him, but if you make a mistake, he'll kill you.

Surprisingly, I don't have a lot of trouble with Billy Williams, who is a good hitter. I keep the ball in on him.

He's a free swinger who likes the ball away. He once hit a home run off me on a ball over his head.

Ernie Banks is a good fast-ball hitter, and still a very tough hitter. I try to throw him breaking balls away.

I get Willie McCovey out pretty good throwing him fast balls up and in. If you don't throw hard you can't do that against him. Then you just have to go with your best pitch.

Jim Ray Hart has learned to back away from the ball inside after he was hit a few times. You still have to throw him fast balls inside, then come outside with breaking balls.

When Tommy Davis was in our league, I got him out fairly well throwing him sliders and fast balls away.

Ed Kranepool gets his hits off me, but he hasn't hurt me and I don't worry about him too much. I try to keep the ball away from him.

Another Met, Ron Swoboda, I get out exceptionally well. I just throw him fast balls, curve balls, anything. I once struck him out four times in a game. He's one of those free swingers and if he's not swinging where you're pitching, you're all right.

I keep the ball in on Pete Rose and he doesn't trouble me too much.

Of course, any of these guys, if you make a mistake they're going to hit it. That's why they're in the big league. They're all good hitters. But I think there's a place you can pitch anyone. You can get a psychological edge on a guy if you get him out consistently. If you can keep a guy wondering if he can hit you, then you're in good shape. Once he builds up his confidence and believes he can hit you, he's going to be a better hitter. When a guy hits you fairly well you bear down a little harder against him and that's when you make a mistake. I think that's what happens when I pitch against Willie Davis.

I think I get the good hitters out more consistently than the not-so-good hitters because I probably concentrate more on the good hitters. I make more mistakes against the seventh-

and eighth-place hitters, and that's bad. In baseball they say never let the bad hitters beat you. The good hitters are going to beat you once in a while.

Sometimes a hitter can outsmart himself. He remembers that the last time you got him out with curve balls away, so this time he's going to sit and wait until he gets the curve ball out there. So you give him three fast balls inside. Next time he might be thinking about those three fast balls and you give him three sliders . . . one . . . two . . . three . . . sit down.

I'll run down a few more of the hitters and how I pitch them, but bear in mind that none of this is foolproof. The good hitter will adjust. You can't pitch him one way, you have to move the ball around.

Bill White: I don't have a lot of trouble with Bill if I make a good pitch. I want to pitch him inside and he knows it. He pulls away sometimes, and when he does I go away with the ball. You can tell what they're expecting after throwing one pitch.

Johnny Callison: A tough hitter for me. I pitch him differently depending on where we're playing. I don't want him pulling the ball in our park. In his park I pitch him inside. I tried pitching him away and found out he hits that ball up into those left-field seats real easy.

Richie Allen: He's strong, but you can get him to chase the ball up high once in a while.

Donn Clendenon: I get him out real well with fast balls inside. He backs off the plate and I come in a little more and he still swings at it.

Willie Stargell: I can get him to chase a bad pitch. He's one of the strongest hitters I know. He hits home runs as far to left field as most right-handed batters.

Tony Gonzalez: A real good hitter. I try to pitch him inside. I make good pitches on him. I'll jam him and break his bat and he still hits the ball over or through the infield.

Rusty Staub: If anybody hurts me on the Astros it's Staub,

again because he's left-handed. He hits me fair, but I don't think it's anything to rave about.

Maury Wills: I don't have any trouble with Maury. I try to throw him high fast balls and let him hit it in the air. He's not strong enough to hit the ball out. When he's batting left-handed he'll hit a lot of fly balls to left field if you get it up and away. The biggest problem is when he gets on base. He's like Lou Brock. You know they're going to go, it's just a question of when. I try not to worry about it. If you worry about it you're going to make a mistake on the hitter. How many times are you going to throw them out anyway? Very seldom. So why worry about them? The best thing to do is keep them off the bases.

This is not meant to be biased, but you'll notice that most of the hitters I mentioned as tops in the league are Negro ballplayers. That's not prejudice, it's fact. And it's not only true of our league. Of the top ten hitters in the American League in 1967, six were Negroes. Of the top ten hitters in the National League, nine were Negroes. That's fifteen out of twenty and there's a reason for that.

It has something to do with Negroes becoming more and more sports-minded. It's a way out of the ghetto, a chance to make a decent living in an area where Negroes are accepted.

Are Negroes better athletes than whites? I don't know. Some people say there is a physiological reason why the fastest runners in track and the highest jumpers in basketball are Negroes, but I don't think that's true. After we had moved into our house in the all-white area of Omaha, I asked my daughter Renee how she liked the neighborhood. She was ten at the time. She said it was all right but there were no colored children there and that colored children were stronger than white children. I laughed to myself. I found it funny . . . and interesting. I thought it odd that she believed that.

Maybe Negroes are better athletes than whites, and maybe there's a reason for that. But I don't think it's physiological.

I think the reason is—maybe it's different now but I know this was true when I was a kid—that the Negro kid devoted more time to sports. There was nothing else to do, so he played ball. I think it goes back to what the white person did as a kid as distinguished from what the Negro did. Maybe the white kid did not do the same thing or maybe the Negro kid did more of it. Take me for example. I played baseball from the time I got up until the time I went to bed.

The white person doesn't have to look to sports to make a good living. There are white people who would have been outstanding athletes if they had stayed with it, but they didn't have to. There were so many opportunities to get into some lucrative business they didn't have to concentrate on baseball. Whereas a Negro with the ability will concentrate most of his efforts toward baseball.

It's the same with music and dancing. That's what Negroes have done for their diversion, they've danced and they've played musical instruments. It was one of the areas that was open to them. Not all Negroes have rhythm or can run fast. I know some Negroes playing baseball who can't run. You know what I can't do? I can't make a radio. But I have a brother who can. But he can't dance.

There's a certain type of person who will become outstanding in whatever he tries. A great baseball player would probably excel in any field he concentrated on. There are successful businessmen who have the competitive drive to be top ballplayers if they had concentrated on it. But these areas are not open to Negroes, so he concentrates on baseball and becomes a top baseball player and many of them might have been successful businessmen if they had the opportunity to concentrate on that.

There were a lot of Negroes playing baseball thirty and forty years ago who would have been great stars in the major leagues, but they weren't given the opportunity. What I am saying is that if the Negro gets the chance, he will excel. He got the chance in baseball and he has excelled. If you give him the same chance in other fields, he will prove he can excel there too.

Jackie Robinson was the first Negro in the major leagues, but he was not the first Negro who was qualified to play in the majors. He just happened to be the first Negro to get the opportunity. It was inevitable that they would get around to it eventually; they just happened to start with Jackie Robinson. Don't get me wrong, I give Robinson all the credit in the world. I have a great deal of admiration for him. He had an awful lot of courage to do what he did. I'm not sure I would have had as much courage in his place. I don't want to detract from what he did, but if it hadn't been Jackie Robinson, it would have been somebody. If Babe Ruth didn't set the home-run record, somebody else would have. If Abner Doubleday hadn't invented baseball (he did, didn't he? Or is that a legend?) somebody else would have.

Somebody was going to invent baseball. Somebody was going to invent television. Somebody was going to discover electricity. Somebody was going to be the first to send a rocket to the moon. Somebody was going to be the first Negro in professional baseball.

What I'm talking about is motivation as opposed to complacency. If a person is so motivated, he's going to do things nobody believed he could do. If you give the Negro the opportunity to make something of himself, he's going to surprise you. When that happens, we'll all be a lot better off.

CHAPTER 18 *NO TIME FOR CRUTCHES*

I heard the crack of the bat and I saw the ball coming at me. It was a dart. I saw it coming but I couldn't move. All my weight was on my leg and I could only stand there and feel it crash with a sickening thud against my right leg, just above the ankle.

I didn't think of the pain at first. All I thought of was the ball rolling away and the runner streaking toward first base and that I had to scramble after the ball and try to throw him out.

Tim McCarver had signaled for a fast ball and I had shaken him off. He put down two fingers for a curve ball. Again I shook him off. Now he put down three fingers, a slider, which was what I wanted to throw.

We were playing the Pirates and Roberto Clemente was the batter. He hits the inside pitch very well so I tried to get the ball away, on the outside part of the plate. I got it away, but not far enough. I got it over the middle of the plate. Two inches farther away and he would not have hit the ball so hard. He might not have hit it at all.

Everything after that happened so fast . . . the crack of the bat . . . the ball smashing against my right leg and rolling away toward shortstop. I wanted to go after it, but I couldn't

If I look like I am in pain, I sure was. Roberto Clemente's line → drive hit me in the right leg. *UPI*

move. Clemente streaked across the bag with a hit as I looked at him, helpless.

Then I felt the pain. It flared up through my leg. I lay down on the infield to see if I could take it any better that way. Doc Bauman, our trainer, came out and sprayed the leg with ethyl chloride to help kill the pain.

"Hey, Doc," I said, "I hate to tell you, but you're spraying in the wrong place."

I thought the pain was someplace else, but Doc was right. He saw the dent in my leg and that's where he sprayed.

"Why don't we just put some tape on it," I suggested. I figured it was just a bruise and I was anxious to get on with the game. When you get hit like that, you're numb. I saw no reason not to continue pitching.

Willie Stargell was the next hitter. I walked him. I was favoring the leg and it affected my control, but I figured I would be all right. Then I got Bill Mazeroski on a pop. I tried to put a little extra pressure on a 3–2 pitch to Donn Clendenon and when I followed through and came down heavily on my right leg, I felt something snap and I tumbled to the ground.

Doc Bauman and Red Schoendienst came running to the mound and Doc helped me limp off the field. As I got to the dugout runway that leads to the clubhouse the pain became more severe. I knew it was serious, but I refused to admit it to myself.

They put me on the training table and Dr. I. C. Middleman, the club physician, came in and ripped my pants leg and began probing around the injured area.

"I think it's broken," he said.

Those were exactly the words I didn't want to hear. "No, it can't be," I argued. That was the first thing that went through my mind, "It can't be." The second was "I wonder how long I'll be out."

◄— Doc Bauman gave me a pain-killer and I stayed in the game.
UPI

Dr. Middleman called for an ambulance to take me to St. Louis Jewish Hospital for X-rays. Curt Flood, who was on the disabled list with an injured shoulder, came with me.

At the hospital they wheeled me into the X-ray room, then they put me in a wheelchair and told me to wait until Dr. Middleman looked at the X-rays. It seemed like hours before he arrived with the bad news.

"It's what I thought," he said. "It's broken."

I guess I knew it all along but I didn't want to think about it, so I'd put it out of my mind. He said Clemente's ball cracked the bone and I snapped it in half on the pitch to Clendenon.

"Will I need a cast?" I asked.

"Yes," Doc said.

That was bad news. I knew a cast meant I'd be out from six to eight weeks. The season would be practically over. I was really depressed.

I wasn't worried about the team being finished. The accident occurred on July 15 and we were four games in front. I was confident the team would do well because we had depth in our pitching staff. Others were not quite so confident. *The Sporting News* had a story of the accident and a picture of me on the ground and the headline "Did Card Flag Dream Go Down With Gibson?" A reporter asked me if I thought the team would go down the drain with me out. That got me angry.

"No, I don't," I said. "This is too good a team to be hurt by losing one man."

Frankly, my main concern was a selfish one. Naturally, I wanted the team to win the pennant, but I knew we would . . . even without me. My main concern was there goes my year. I had started out pretty good. My record at the time of the injury was 10–6, and considering my history of doing better in the second half I thought I could win 22 or 23, particularly with such a good team. I was in the prime of my career and another big year would put me in a pretty good income bracket. In this game you have to make it when you can.

I guess I was a bit testy with reporters during that period. I think they should have been a little more understanding but they weren't. The cast was on only three days when one of them asked me when I was going to pitch. How should I know?

Feeling the way I did, I got tired answering the same questions over and over, so I made myself a little sign and hung it around my neck every time I went into the clubhouse. It said:

"1—Yes, it's off!!! (the cast).

"2—No, it doesn't hurt!

"3—I'm not supposed to walk on it for one week!!

"4—I don't know how much longer!

"5—Ask Doc Bauman!

"6—Ask Doc Middleman!"

I did it as a joke, but some of the reporters didn't take it that way and I was criticized for it.

While I sat by watching, my teammates did pretty well without me. Six weeks after I broke my leg they increased their lead to 11½. The team was going good and they really didn't need me and maybe that's what made me so depressed. I was glad they were winning, but subconsciously you don't like to think of them not needing you. You want to go out there and win some games because it means a lot to you, and in this case it hurt me even more because the team was going so well, scoring so many runs. I never saw so many runs scored in my life and I wasn't able to take advantage of it. They were scoring 8, 9 runs a game. I've got to win some of those games and here I am sitting back with a broken leg.

They really played great ball while I was out. Everybody was doing his job. The pitching was tremendous, which didn't surprise me. The only one who surprised me was Steve Carl-

I was out seven weeks with a broken bone. That sign on me answers all the questions. *UPI*

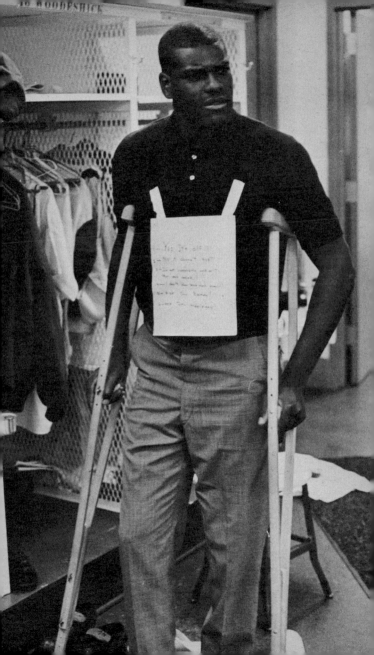

ton. I knew he could throw hard and that he had a good
curve ball. I didn't know if he had enough experience to
develop a good pitching sense, but he did. He won 14 games
and improved maybe 100 percent over the previous year.
Briles also won 14, which didn't surprise me because Nellie
pitched so well; in 1966 he just didn't have much luck. Dick
Hughes won 16, but I always knew he had good stuff.

Orlando Cepeda was unbelievable. He had the kind of year
Bill White had for us in 1964 and deserved his award as Most
Valuable Player. There were times when nobody else was
hitting and Cha-Cha carried the club by himself. Our pitchers
would allow 2 runs and Cha-Cha would knock in 3. He helped
keep up the team spirit too. We'd win a game and Cepeda
would come in leading the cheers and climb up on a chair
and begin to shout.

"We're the Cardinals."

And everybody would answer, "yeah."

"We're the best."

"Yeah."

"We're the champs."

"Yeah."

"El Birdos."

"Yeah."

The papers picked up the "El Birdos" and began using
it in headlines and stories and the next thing you knew somebody was selling buttons that said "El Birdos."

I want to pay tribute to Julian Javier, who may be the
most underrated player in our league. He was a great player
in 1967. He batted .281 and drove in 64 runs and made some
defensive plays you could hardly believe. You never hear
much about Hoolie, but in my opinion he's a better second
baseman than Bill Mazeroski, and that's giving Maz his due.
Hoolie has better range in either direction because he's faster
than Maz, and I think he makes the double play better.

Another important factor in our success was the shift of

Mike Shannon to third base. When Red announced he was doing it, I thought it was a horrible idea. Mike is a good outfielder with a terrific arm and a good hitter, but I doubted he could do the job as a third baseman. But we had Roger Maris for right field and we couldn't make a trade for a good third baseman, so Red tried Shannon there. Mike worked hard and made himself into an adequate third baseman, which is to his credit. He also helped at bat with 77 RBI.

Nobody got close to us after the early part of August. We turned back every team that made a run at us. In one string we had a four-game series with Chicago and three games with Cincinnati, Atlanta, and San Francisco. All of these clubs were on the move when we met them and we cooled them off by winning the series against each one.

The team that gave us the biggest scare was the Chicago Cubs. I underestimated them. So did everybody else. I thought they'd end up in the second division because I didn't think their pitching was that strong. Even after they stayed up there for half a season, I thought they wouldn't hold up, but they surprised me. They came into St. Louis just two games out of first and we beat them 3 out of 4 and that broke their back.

All this made me more anxious to get back in there. The cast came off my leg after three weeks, but I wasn't able to do anything except walk around on crutches. Doc didn't want me to put any weight on the leg. After three days I was so impatient I threw away the crutches. It didn't hurt and I saw no reason to use the crutches. Three days later Dr. Middleman said I could get rid of the crutches and start working out. I think he knew I already had. He told me I could throw on the sidelines, but not off the mound. I took infield practice and ran in the outfield to get my leg strong again.

Doc gave me the OK to make the next trip to California and Houston, cautioning me that I could pitch batting practice and do anything I wanted except pitch in a game. I couldn't see the logic in that. I suppose he figured you put more into it when you're bearing down in a game than when you're pitching batting practice.

Now I was really getting irritable, asking Red when I could pitch and running upstairs to plead my case with our general manager, Stan Musial.

"It's almost September," I argued. "I'm ready. When am I going to pitch?"

Stan told me to be patient, that there was no sense risking reinjury, particularly since the team was going so well. It would be silly to take a chance. I asked him to take a chance for me, not for the team. It meant a lot to me. I wanted to win some more games. I was thinking of the money. That's what we're in this game for. If you have a good year you get a raise. If you don't have a good year you don't get a raise, and I didn't think a 10—6 record was a very good year.

On September 6, exactly seven weeks and four days after my injury, Doc Bauman said he thought my leg was all right and that I should be pitching. I went right to Musial, who said he was returning me to the active list the next day. What's more, I was to start against the Mets. There were only 3½ weeks left in the season and I intended to make the most of them.

I never get nervous before a game, but I was like a schoolboy on September 7, 1967. I was leery about shoving off the mound and landing hard on my right leg with my vigorous follow-through. But I knew I had to find out once and for all. There was no doubt in my mind that I would be able to come back and pitch. In 1962 I had broken the same bone when my spikes caught while I was taking batting practice. The only difference was that it happened with a week left in the season and I didn't have to test it until the following spring. My concern this time was that I might be rushing things.

After the first inning I knew I would be all right. I pitched until the sixth, then I was removed. We had a big lead and I got credit for the victory, but they hit me pretty hard. That didn't worry me. I was only interested in how the leg would feel and in pitching myself back into shape. I was all right on the first count. On the second, I knew I needed work.

I was sore all over when the game ended. It was like starting spring training all over.

Red put me on a schedule of starting every fifth game. My next start came against the Phillies on September 12. I pitched shutout ball for 6 2/3 innings, then Larry Jaster came in to save the shutout and my twelfth victory. I was feeling much better.

My turn came up again on September 18, and as luck would have it we needed one victory to clinch the pennant. This was not a setup for me, it just worked out that way. I pitched nine strong innings against the Phillies. We were National League champions!

It made me feel good to pitch the pennant-clincher, but I was happier that I had gone nine innings. I was still far from satisfied. I had a lot to make up for. I wanted several more starts before the World Series. I had to settle for two more.

While we were playing out the season and getting ready for the World Series, the American League was having the kind of dog-fight usually associated with the National League. They came down to the last two days with four teams still in it—Minnesota, Detroit, Chicago, and Boston. We were keeping close watch on that race . . . and rooting. Not that we favored one team over another or figured one team was easier than the other three. We thought we could beat all of them. But we were rooting against the Red Sox . . . rather, we were rooting for money. We wanted the big ball park in Minnesota, Chicago, or Detroit because the World Series share would be bigger. Wouldn't you know it? Boston won.

I had finished the season with a 13–7 record, but I tried to put that out of my mind and concentrate on the World Series. Here was my chance to turn a disappointing season into a rewarding one.

The carnival atmosphere that usually prevails during a World Series was missing for me. Once you're in the Series, the pressure is off in a way. There is never a loser in a World Series, just two winners, one bigger than the other. You're still going to go home with a healthy check and, since you've won the pennant, a salary increase for the following year is almost automatic.

For me it was different this time. For me the 1967 season began on Wednesday, October 4, the day of the first game of the World Series. I was determined to make it a good season.

We flew into Boston the day before the Series opener. It was a town gone mad. I suppose you couldn't blame them. They hadn't won a pennant in twenty-one years and they came from ninth place the year before to win on the last day of the season. I just think they got a little carried away.

On Tuesday we had the inevitable meeting to go over the inevitable scouting reports. I don't know why I waste my time listening to these things. One of the gems I heard was that you could get one of their hitters out with a changeup inside. Well, for Pete's sake, you wouldn't throw your grandmother a changeup inside. I shouldn't be too critical of scouting reports. They actually helped me in the Series—not our report on

Boston, their report on us. Somebody got hold of their report and printed it in the paper. It said Gibson was a high-fast-ball pitcher—which everybody knew—who didn't have a good curve ball or slider. Thank you for that, Mr. Scout. The Red Sox went up there believing I didn't have a curve ball or slider and most of my strikeouts came on breaking balls.

When we finished with the report, we went out on the field for a light workout and to get acquainted with Fenway Park. The reporters were around there like locusts. Sometimes I think they assign ten reporters to cover each player in the World Series.

They bombarded me with questions. The three most frequently asked were: How is your leg? How are you going to pitch to Carl Yastrzemski? Are you concerned about the short left-field wall?

My answers were: The leg is as strong as ever; I didn't know how I would pitch Yastrzemski, I would find out when I faced him, and even if I did know I wouldn't tell you; and I wasn't concerned about the short left-field wall because the hitters wouldn't pull the ball on me, and if they tried to pull me that would be to my advantage because all I'd have to do is keep it away and they'd pop it up.

The night before the first game I relaxed by going out to dinner, then to see Cannonball Adderly, the jazz saxophonist. I love modern jazz. It is one of my hobbies. Listening to music is one of the ways I like to relax. There were six of us—Orlando Cepeda, Al Jackson, me, and our wives. I had a glass of champagne. I wasn't celebrating in advance. I never drink hard liquor. The only thing I will take is ginger ale or a glass of champagne on occasion. We returned to the hotel and I went to sleep before midnight.

There was no particular excitement before the first game, despite the pomp and ceremony, all the reporters and photographers and celebrities. I had been through all this before, so there were no World Series jitters. I had to wonder if there

This was the opening game of the 1967 World Series. *UPI*

were any among the Red Sox, many of whom were playing in their first Series.

My pitching opponent was Jose Santiago, a righthander who had won 12 and lost 4 during the year. We posed for the usual pregame pictures without saying much to each other. Then I went down to the bullpen to warm up.

I was really blazing the ball in the bullpen. I felt strong and loose, but after a couple of pitches, on the mound, I didn't think I was throwing as hard as I was in the bullpen. I got through the first inning, then asked McCarver about it.

"I'm not throwing real good, am I?" I said.

"Oh no," Tim corrected. "You're throwing real good."

I made a lot of bad pitches in that first game, but fortunately only one hurt me. In the third inning I was ahead of Santiago, no balls, 2 strikes, and I hung a curve ball and he hit it over the left-field wall to tie the score, 1–1. It was a mistake, a perfect home-run pitch. I just got careless and didn't dig down on the ball hard enough and it came up there big as a balloon. Later, I was asked if it disturbed me that the home run came on an 0–2 pitch and was hit by the pitcher. It always disturbs me when I give up a home run, no matter who hits it or what the count is.

The home run was all they got. I tired in the last two innings and threw nothing but fast balls and sliders for fear of hanging another curve ball with a 1-run lead. We scored 2 runs, both by Lou Brock and both driven in by Roger Maris with ground balls to the right side.

I gave up only six hits and struck out ten and handled Yastrzemski, their best hitter, fairly easily. In four at-bats, he fouled out, grounded to the second baseman, and hit two routine fly balls to left field. After the first game I had no reason to alter my original prediction: the Cardinals in five.

In the second game we got to see the pitcher everybody was talking about, Jim Lonborg, their ace. Dick Hughes pitched for us.

Charline gave me vocal support from the stands.   *UPI*

Lonborg was good, very good, but I didn't think he was a superman or anything. We got only one hit off him in that second game. We have a good-hitting club and I didn't think Lonborg, or anybody else for that matter, could stop us the way he did. In truth, we hit the ball hard against him, but without luck. I figured we'd get him next time. They evened the Series, one game apiece, but I still believed we would win the next three games in our park.

My impression of Lonborg was that he had great control and a good breaking ball, but he didn't throw that hard. When a guy wins 22 games, as he did, you expect you'll see him and say, "Boy, can he blow." Lonborg doesn't throw that hard. He mixes his pitches well, but he didn't impress us as much as we thought he would.

With his first pitch of the game, Lonborg set the stage for what was to become a big misunderstanding throughout the Series. He threw one that separated Lou Brock from his cap. Lou had smacked four hits in the first game and stolen two bases and generally disrupted them with his baserunning. I guess Lonborg was delivering his calling card, trying to establish right from the start that he was the boss.

I got up on the top step of the dugout and yelled at him, "You'll get your turn at bat, too." I doubt if he heard me. You never hear that stuff. A guy can be cursing you or calling you a sweetheart, you never know it. All you know is that he's saying something.

There was an exchange of words between our bench and theirs, but nothing out of the ordinary. This kind of stuff goes on all the time during the season. But in a World Series everything is magnified.

There was no bitter feeling between the two teams, most of that existed only in the newspapers. Sometimes I think the reporters get more personally involved than the players. We felt it had been so long since Boston had anything to cheer about that they tried to make a big deal out of everything, like the Cardinals were mad at the Red Sox and the Red Sox were mad at the Cardinals. I can't recall being mad at anybody or anybody being mad at me. Just because I said we'd beat them in five and George Scott said he'd knock me out in five innings, that doesn't mean we were mad at each other. We're professional athletes, we're supposed to think that way.

Here's how a thing like that gets started. Before the Series a reporter asked me what I thought about Yastrzemski. I said he's in the other league, so I don't think about him very much. The next day in the paper, in big headlines, it said: "Gibson Doesn't Think Much of Yaz." Now what can you do about that?

Another thing that appeared in the papers was a quote from Lonborg that he intended to brush Brock back with his first pitch. In the first inning of the third game, Nelson Briles hit Yastrzemski in the leg with a pitch. Now I can't look into Nellie's mind, but I know he reads the newspapers. I also know Yastrzemski hit two home runs in the second game. And I also know one and one makes two.

The umpires got together with the two managers and said all right, now you're even, let's cut out this throwing stuff.

I was confident Nellie would beat them and he did. He tired late in the game, but we had enough of a cushion to win, 5–2.

I felt good warming up for the fourth game, but for some reason I wasn't throwing very hard. I knew it would be a struggle. I would have to pitch a different type of ball game. My teammates picked me up and helped make it easy for me by scoring 4 runs in the first inning off Santiago. With that kind of lead, you can do things. You can get by even if you don't have a good breaking ball or your best control. We won, 6–0, and I gave them only four hits. It's funny. I had better stuff in the first game, but you couldn't tell it by the statistics except in strikeouts. I had only six in the fourth game.

Yastrzemski got two hits—a single and a double—and in the ninth inning he went from second to third on a fly ball

with his team behind by 6 runs, which struck me as odd. He later told reporters, "If Gibson was going to pitch a shutout, he was going to have to earn it."

Yaz also paid me a compliment. He told Eddie Bressoud, "He's a good pitcher because he beat us and he didn't have good stuff."

When the game ended, Cha-Cha led the charge into the clubhouse.

"El Birdos," he shouted.

"Yeah."

"El Birdos."

"Yeah."

"El Birdos."

"Yeah."

"Three games to one."

"Yeah."

"Do you want to go back to Boston?"

"No."

Cepeda's enthusiasm notwithstanding, we were going back to Boston. I thought Steve Carlton would shut them out in the fifth game and we could go home without having to go back to Boston. I was packed and ready to leave. I was sure I had pitched my last game of the year.

Steve pitched well enough to win, he just had no luck. He gave them three hits and 1 run through six innings, then left for a pinch-hitter. Again our relief pitching failed to hold them. Jim Lonborg pitched another strong game to beat us, 3–1. We were going back to Boston, a little down about having to make the trip.

When Hughes got beat again in the sixth game, the Series was all tied at three games each and I had to go to work one more time.

It was a one-game season and the newspapers played it for all it was worth. They tried to build it up as a showdown between Lonborg and myself. I didn't see it quite that way. I

This one felt real good—a home run off Jim Lonborg in the seventh game. *UPI* wasn't trying to prove anything. I just wanted to win the game, get the biggest share of the money, and go home.

The night before the big game Charline and I and a few friends went to the Jazz Workshop, where Les McCann, the great jazz pianist and a good friend of mine, was playing. We stayed until a little after eleven and I was in bed by twelve. I had trouble sleeping. I wasn't thinking about the game, I often have trouble sleeping. It seems every time I roll over during the night, I wake up and can't go back to sleep.

We were staying in a motel in Quincy, a suburb of Boston. At nine on the morning of the game, we went into the restaurant for breakfast. There must have been seventy people waiting to be served and only two waitresses to serve them. I ordered scrambled eggs and ham, toast and coffee. About 50 minutes later, the waitress came with some burnt toast. She wasn't trying to sabotage us and send us to the park hungry because we were the enemy, she was just too busy. By then it was time to catch the bus to the ballpark, so we got up and left without eating.

A hungry ballplayer is a good ballplayer, they say, but this was ridiculous. My stomach was growling. As usual I had something to complain about on the bus. Bob Broeg, the sportswriter for the St. Louis *Post-Dispatch*, was the only one who showed any sympathy for me.

"Stop the bus," he told the driver when we got downtown, "I'll get off and get Hoot a couple of sandwiches."

The bus pulled up at the players' entrance of Fenway Park and although it was still three hours before gametime, the sidewalks were jammed with people. As the guys were getting off the bus, I announced, as I usually do when I'm scheduled to pitch, "OK, you guys, let's get 'em. This may be the biggest game of the year." I couldn't resist using the line again. It was good for a laugh.

Before every Series game, Mr. Busch, the owner of the Cardinals, came through the clubhouse to wish us luck. This time he stopped by my locker, pulled up a stool, and talked awhile. Nothing special, just small talk. He wished me luck and left. He appeared to be more nervous than I was.

I was dressed and ready to go out to take batting practice when Bob Broeg arrived with two ham-and-egg sandwiches. I ate one and saved the other for after the game. I was so hungry, it tasted like steak. My hunger satisfied, I went out onto the field and into a mob of reporters. Normally, I don't like to talk to reporters before I pitch, but this was going to be the last time for at least five months, so I answered their questions.

"What do you think of Yastrzemski?"

Oh no. Not again.

I told them I thought Yastrzemski was a good ballplayer. He proved it during the season with the kind of year he had, so he must be a good ballplayer. But I think the reporters tried to make too much of him. We have lots of good ballplayers in our league. They wanted me to compare him with guys like Mays and Mantle and Aaron and Frank Robinson, and I said I couldn't do that. These guys have been great ballplayers for ten years or more. After ten years, then ask me about Yastrzemski and I'll be able to look back at what he did and then I can compare him with these others guys.

There really was nothing more I could say. He hit a few home runs in the Series, but he never hurt me. I think he might be a fast-ball hitter. If I can get the fast ball where I want it, he's not going to hit it. If I make a mistake, he'll hit it. That's all there is to it. He's a good hitter, but when I got the ball where I wanted it, he popped it up to shortstop.

The scouting report said pitch him inside in Boston to keep him from popping for that short left-field wall. So he hit 2 home runs into the right-field bleachers. The guy hit 44 home runs during the season and I figure he didn't hit all of them to left field. Besides, I don't believe you should change the way you pitch because of the ball park. I moved the ball around on him and when I made a good pitch outside, he popped it up.

As I started to warm up, I was a little concerned about whether I was going to have good stuff. It was only the second time all season that I was pitching with three days' rest. I figured I would be strong for about six innings. If I thought I was going to be tired, I imagined Lonborg would be more tired pitching with only two days' rest. I had gone through that in 1964, but I was luckier than Lonborg. I had a big lead to work with right from the start. I watched Lonborg throw and he didn't look any more tired than he did the other two games, but you could see he wasn't throwing well.

I told the reporters that I would probably be strong for six or seven innings and that Lonborg would probably start getting tired around the third. I was right on both counts. I started by striking out seven of the first twelve batters, then George Scott got the first hit, a triple to center. He hit a pitch so far outside it was a ball. I had pitched him inside in the first game and he got two hits, so we decided to keep the ball away, but he is so strong and hit it so hard I thought it was going out of the park. He scored when Javier's relay went into the dugout. By that time we had 4 runs and much of the pressure was off. One of those runs came on a home run I hit over the left-center-field fence that really felt good. We put the game out of reach with 3 more in the sixth, which came just at the right time because I was getting tired. I didn't think I could finish, especially after they roughed me up a little in the eighth.

Rico Petrocelli opened with a double. I got behind him and that's the worst thing you can do when you're not throwing good. I had to come in with a pitch over the plate and he got his double. When I wild-pitched him to third, Billy Muffett, our pitching coach, came to the mound. I didn't think he was coming to get me out. He wasn't.

"Bear down," he said, then went back into the dugout. I walked the next batter, Dalton Jones, and the Boston crowd was beginning to come alive and I was struggling. I decided to junk the fast ball and go with the slider. I fooled Norm

I was tiring fast in the seventh game, but Red didn't come to get me—just to give me a breather.   *UPI*

Siebern with one and he hit into a force play, a run scoring. Joe Foy hit a slider off the end of his bat to first base for another force play. And another slider got Mike Andrews on a ground ball. As I came off the field I was so tired I didn't think I would finish.

"How you doing?" Schoendienst asked me.

"OK," I said.

"Let's try to get this thing over with."

That's what I wanted to do more than anything in the world. I started the ninth inning getting behind Yastrzemski, 2–0, and had to lay it in there. That's all I was trying to do, get it over the plate and keep it down so he wouldn't hit a home run. He whacked it to right field for a single.

I had a 5-run lead, but I needed help. I got it right away. Ken Harrelson tried to pull a slider and hit a high hopper to third base and Hoolie turned that double play over at second base faster than anybody I've ever seen. That was the breather I needed.

I threw harder to George Scott than I had all game because I knew he was the last man and there was no reason to save anything. I threw a couple of fast balls and he fouled them back. Then I threw him a couple of sliders outside for balls. The next pitch was a slider high and inside, a bad pitch. He hesitated. He wasn't going to swing at it. Then he swung because it was too tempting. He missed.

McCarver ran out and shook my hand and shouted, "Helluva game, Hoot." Cepeda came over from first base. We started slapping and beating each other. I ran down the dugout steps and policemen were trying to keep the kids away. Somebody grabbed Cepeda's cap, but he chased him and got it back. I didn't give them a chance to get mine. I took it off and held it in my hand.

The clubhouse was the usual victory mob scene of reporters and photographers and champagne bottles being uncorked and the bubbly stuff going all over the floor.

We did it again!   *UPI*

Reporters—forty or fifty of them—backed me into my locker and began firing questions at me. One of them was reading from a book and saying, "Do you know you tied a World Series record for most consecutive complete games? And that you tied Christy Mathewson's record of allowing only fourteen hits in three World Series games?"

"Well . . . er . . . no," I said. "I haven't got that book."

All of a sudden I saw Les McCann standing on a stool and brandishing his right fist and shouting, "Black Power! Black Power!" I didn't know where he came from or how he got in there. No doubt he was saying it for my benefit. He just wanted me to know he was there. A reporter asked me who he was and I said, "Les McCann, a friend of mine."

The reporter said, "Oh," and went on asking questions while I sipped from a bottle of champagne.

Somebody told me I had won the *Sport* magazine Corvette as the outstanding performer in the Series. I was happy to hear that, but I honestly believed Lou Brock deserved it. Without him we couldn't have won. He was on base all the time and he completely upset them with his running.

I was happy and I was tired and I wanted to go home and rest. I was glad we won and that it was over and that my season was a success.

An hour later the champagne was still flowing and the questions were still coming and Orlando Cepeda was still standing on a stool and shouting:

"We're the champions of the world."

"Yeah."

"We're the Cardinals."

"Yeah."

"El Birdos."

"Yeah."

CHAPTER 20 *LBJ AND ME*

The World Series was over a month and I thought I had reached all the peaks of excitement in my life. Then one day I received a letter. At the top it said simply:

> The Office of the President of the United States
> The White House
> Washington, D.C.

Charline and I were cordially invited to attend a dinner at the White House in honor of Premier Eisaku Sato of Japan on November 14. Rarely am I ever impressed or do I get excited about things, but this was the most thrilling thing that ever happened to me. Imagine me, a poor kid from the ghetto of Omaha, having dinner at the White House with the President of the United States!

I was on a busy schedule of banquets and appearances, but I canceled everything to go to Washington.

I imagine everybody has an idea, from what they read in newspapers and magazines, of what it would be like to go to the White House and mingle with people who might be considered high society. I know I did. I thought it might be stuffy and very formal and that I would feel out of place. I was wrong. The people I met were all down to earth. It was quite different than I expected.

The guests were a cross-section of people from all walks of life. Among them were Roger Blough, chairman of the United States Steel Corporation; Governor Otto Kerner of Illinois; Frank Stanton, president of the Columbia Broadcasting System; baseball commissioner William Eckert; and one of my favorite actors, Kirk Douglas.

Before the dinner there was a cocktail party and reception and a receiving line, where I shook hands with President Johnson. He said, "Hello, how are you?" He had just returned from a long tour and his face was drawn and he looked very tired. I could sympathize with him. I know all about those long road trips.

I was introduced to Premier Sato, who took my hand and measured it against his. He said something which I couldn't understand, but I guessed he was making reference to the size of my hand.

Vice President Humphrey greeted me cordially. He is a great baseball fan and he congratulated me on the World Series. He noticed that he and I were the only ones in the room wearing blue shirts with our tuxedos and he commented on that.

"We're the only ones here who dress with any class," he said.

I had met President Johnson once before, at the All-Star game in Washington in 1962. I was in the hotel lobby and Earl Battey introduced us.

"I'd like you to meet the Vice President," he said.

After he left, I asked Earl if he was the vice president of the Washington Senators.

"No," Earl said to my embarrassment, "he's the Vice President of the United States."

The dinner at the White House was exceptionally good, or maybe I thought it was because it was the White House, I don't know. But I did enjoy the meal and the different types of wine we had to drink. White wine with fish, red wine with the main course, and champagne after dinner.

When dinner was over we were directed to a large room that looked like a lobby. An orchestra was set up and there was a large dance floor. We danced for an hour or two, then everybody left. I think Charline and I and Kirk Douglas and his wife were the last to leave. It seemed like we closed the doors of the White House.

All in all it was one of the most memorable experiences in my life, something I'll never forget. And when my girls get old enough to appreciate my experience, they'll never forget it either.

Looking back on the '67 series, a number of other memories stand out. After the last game, we boarded a charter plane for St. Louis and went from the airport directly to Stan Musial's restaurant, where we had a big victory celebration with the whole Cardinal organization there, scouts, office help, everybody. We had a ball. Nelson Briles sang a couple of songs and squeezed an accordion while I played the keyboard and Dick Hughes yodeled.

There were speeches and a lot of nice things said about me. The way I felt was that a pitcher is only as good as his team, I don't care how much stuff he has. He can pitch a shutout and if his team doesn't score, what does he get? An 0–0 tie.

The party broke up about eight and Charline and I went back to our hotel. It wasn't until then that it all hit me. "Hey," I said, "I just realized, we won 4 games and I won 3 of them."

"That's what I've been trying to tell you," she said.

The Series seemed to drag on so long, and I was thinking of one game at a time, so it just escaped me that I had won 3. All I knew was that we had finally won 4 and that the fourth one had been a long time coming.

It seemed there was one party after another for the next two or three days. Then I had to leave to go to New York to pick up my Corvette and appear on the Ed Sullivan Show. Lou Brock was also on the show. He couldn't wait to see me. It seemed that St. Louis radio station KMOX had decided that since it was between Lou and me for the Corvette, they would

give a car to whomever didn't win it. They called Lou and told him about it and asked him what kind of car he wanted. Jokingly, Lou said, "An El Dorado." They said, "OK, you've got it." So he wound up with a $12,000 automobile, not bad for a consolation prize.

We left New York and headed for Omaha. I was anxious to get home, to see the children and to rest. But there was no rest for the weary. They had a big reception for me—"Bob Gibson Day"—with parades, speeches, and presentations.

Rodney Wead, who has been my closest friend since childhood and who is active in civic affairs in Omaha, picked me up and we made the rounds of elementary, junior high, and high schools in the ghetto. I visited Kellom, my old grade school, and Technical, my old high school. At each school my message was the same. I urged the kids to stay in school and to work hard and emphasized that if I had not remained in school I never would have had time to make myself into a ballplayer. I would have had to work.

There was a luncheon in my honor in the city auditorium and at Creighton University, Governor Norbert Tiemann, who once got a hit off me in a summer-league game, made me honorary governor of Nebraska. Mayor A. V. Sorenson made me honorary mayor of Omaha. And Father Linn, president of Creighton, made me honorary university president.

"Now that I'm honorary governor," I told the students of Creighton, "I think I'll repeal the new sales and income tax. And now that I'm honorary mayor I think I'll inaugurate an open-housing ordinance. And being honorary president of Creighton, classes are dismissed for the day."

At Lake School, in the heart of the ghetto, the first-graders carried a homemade sign with a picture of an arm and the words "The Arm That Cracked The Red Sox." They presented me with a flower-planter made from a barrel. On a stand were a baseball glove and ball, both gold-plated. They also gave me a plastic key to the school, which was also golden. I was touched by it all.

Norbert Tiemann is governor of Nebraska. I remember when he got a hit off me on the sandlots.

The next few months were hectic ones, and happily so. After the 1964 Series I did very little in the way of endorsements and appearances. In 1967 I made about twenty times as much money during the winter as I did in '64. All this is due to Sandy Bain, who has helped me tremendously. Sandy is vice president of Sportsplan and Marty Glickman is president, and they have been handling my public relations and appearances.

Through them I have made appearances on the "Tonight" show, the Joey Bishop show, the Pat Boone show, the Woody Woodbury show, and "To Tell The Truth." I did commercials for Fairmont Dairies and General Electric, made a movie for the President's Council on Physical Fitness, and did clinics in New York and Puerto Rico for Eastern Air Lines. I also did an episode of the "Gentle Ben" television series, which I really enjoyed. My role was to instruct a boy, Mark, how to be a good sportsman. I liked it so much I would consider trying my hand at movies if the opportunity presented itself.

It was a busy winter, and of all the things I did and the memories I have, the two that stand out are my visit to the White House and "Bob Gibson Day" in Omaha. As mementoes, I have in the basement of my house the invitation to the White House and a plaque I received from the students of Tech High. It says:

"Be it known that in recognition of his outstanding achievement in the field of athletics . . . in appreciation of the honor which he has brought to this school, this community and himself by his conduct both on and off the playing field; in tribute to his personification of the traits and ideals of hard work, dedication, sportsmanship and self-sacrifice; the student body of Omaha Technical High School do, on this 17th day of October, 1967, hereby present an award of merit to a superb athlete, fine gentleman, world champion and fellow Trojan, Bob Gibson."

CHAPTER 21 *LIKE EVERYBODY ELSE*

Where am I going? As far as baseball is concerned I think I have another five years as a starting pitcher and then two or three more as a spot starter and reliever.

I think eventually I'm going to have to become a different type of pitcher than I am now. Right now I'm primarily a fast-ball pitcher and everything I throw works off the fast ball. Later, when I lose a little speed, I'm probably going to have to resort to more breaking balls and changeups and use the fast ball only once in a while. It doesn't worry me. I'm confident I'll still be a winning pitcher, like Robin Roberts, who became primarily a breaking-ball pitcher when he got older. I'm not throwing as hard now as I used to, but my control is better and I know more about pitching.

What I'm saying is I think I can pitch until I'm about forty. It's not impossible. You can pitch a long time if you take care of yourself . . . and I take care of myself.

After I'm through playing? I really don't know. If I stay in baseball it would have to be as a manager, not a coach. Coaches don't get paid enough for all the traveling they do. I think I could find something I liked better than traveling all over the country.

I'm not even sure I'd like to be a manager, but it doesn't

matter because I doubt if I'll ever get the opportunity. It's going to be a long time before there are any Negro managers. I think Bill White would make a good manager if he wanted to be one, but any Negro manager is going to have problems. Everybody is going to be watching him, waiting for him to make a mistake. Everybody makes mistakes, but people are going to make twice as much out of it if he makes one. There's enough pressure in baseball already and a manager is going to get second-guessed enough without having to put up with that kind of added stress. How many people are that thick-skinned?

I doubt if my future is in baseball, but I would like to stay in sports in some capacity, maybe broadcasting. I think I'd like that. I have a weekly radio and television show on station WOW in Omaha and I did the color on Creighton's basketball games. I don't know for sure if my future will be in Omaha, but I would like it to be.

I can't see myself fifteen years from now. I don't know what I will be doing. All I'm interested in is when that time comes, my family will have financial security. I have already taken steps toward that end.

Through my wife's civic activities in Omaha as a member of the Human Relations Board and the Panel of American Women, she has come in contact with many people. One of them is Norman Hahn, president of the American Natural Gas Co. Through Charline I met Norman and we have become very close friends and business associates. He is helping me prepare for my future.

One day Norm said, "I don't want to be nosy, but you aren't saving much money as far as taxes are concerned, are you?"

I admitted I wasn't because I didn't have many investments and I had no businesses, although I had been looking for some.

"I'd like to go into business with you," Norm said. "I don't know what we could do, but we could do something."

I said fine and Norm went to work. He introduced me to many important people in Omaha. He got one the largest accounting firms in the country to handle my taxes. He introduced me to a stockbroker to handle my investments. And he arranged for some of the top lawyers in Omaha to help me with my legal affairs.

In June of 1967, Norm and I and three others formed the Cardinal Realty Corp. We plan to expand into other businesses and, thanks to Norm, I feel my future is secure. Meeting Norman Hahn was one of the high points in my life.

It is not my future, however, but the future of the Negro people that concerns me.

Things must get better and they must get better soon. How it's going to happen is an immense question. Nobody has the answer. I know it's not going to happen by having lunch and forming committees.

I think the best thing I can do is be an example as an athlete. People look up to you as an athlete, they pay attention to what you say. If I were not an athlete, I'm sure I would be out throwing rocks the same as a lot of others. There are a lot of ways to set an example and I feel my way is playing baseball and behaving in such a way as to have people look at me as an individual, not as a baseball player or a Negro.

Baseball is great and I am grateful for my ability to play the game, but other than being a ballplayer, all I am is another guy. I would much rather be known as Bob Gibson, great American, than Bob Gibson, great baseball player.

The day-to-day things that are happening in this country are far from encouraging, yet I can still hope. Without hope there is nothing.

I hope for the equality of all mankind and for the acceptance of all people by all people. Less than twenty-five years ago I couldn't play in the major leagues. Less than ten years ago, I couldn't stay in the same hotel in St. Petersburg with the rest of my teammates. Less than two years ago, I couldn't have moved into an all-white neighborhood in one of Omaha's most exclusive sections.

I hope that my children—and all children—can grow up and reach the utmost of their capabilities without anybody trying to hold them back because of their color or their religion or their last name.

I hope that my children will be able to say, "I can qualify for that job and it's not because I am Bob Gibson's daughter. It's because I am Renee Gibson or Annette Gibson, citizen of the United States, just like everybody else."

Me and my girls, Renee on the left, and Annette.
OMAHA WORLD-HERALD